THE HOUSE ON THE ROCK

THE HOUSE ON THE ROCK

CHARLES SELL

While this book is intended for the reader's personal enjoyment and profit, it is also intended for group study. A Leader's Guide with Victor Multiuse Transparency Masters is available from your local bookstore or from the publisher.

A DIVISION OF SCRIPTURE PRESS PUBLICATIONS INC.
USA CANADA ENGLAND

Unless otherwise noted, Scripture quotations are from the *Holy Bible: New International Version,* © 1973, 1978, 1984, International Bible Society. Used by permission of Zondervan Bible Publishers. Quotations marked NASB are from *New American Standard Bible,* © the Lockman Foundation 1960, 1962, 1963, 1968, 1971, 1972, 1973, 1975, 1977.

Recommended Dewey Decimal Classification: 301.42

Suggested Subject Heading: FAMILY

Library of Congress Catalog Card Number: 86-63152

ISBN: 0-89693-048-3

© 1987 by SP Publications, Inc. All rights reserved. Printed in the United States of America. No part of this book may be used or reproduced in any manner whatsoever without written permission except in the case of brief quotations in critical articles and reviews. For information address Victor Books, Wheaton, IL 60187.

CONTENTS

ONE. *When You Need the Wisdom of Solomon* 7

TWO. *From Head to Heart to Habit* 22

THREE. *What* Commit *Meant* 36

FOUR. *Love in a Nuptial Shell* 50

FIVE. *Forever Lovers* 64

SIX. *Love: The Right Stuff* 77

SEVEN. *Intimacy: Close Up* 91

EIGHT. *Sensual Is Sage* 104

NINE. *Improving Your Clash Assets* 118

TEN. *The Ma and Pa Institute of Higher Learning* 129

ELEVEN. *Designer Discipline* 142

TWELVE. *Go with the Grow* 156

Chapter
ONE

WHEN YOU NEED THE WISDOM OF SOLOMON

Wisdom has built her house.
PROVERBS 9:1

A biology professor took a small group of young biologists into the desert for intensive study. Miles from civilization, the vehicle in which they were traveling broke down. The group set out on foot on an estimated three-day trek back to their campus. After two days of hard travel, they reached the summit of a huge sand dune. Thirsty and sunburned, they looked around them. Far off to their right was what appeared to be a lake with small trees surrounding it. The students jumped and screamed for joy. But the teacher, who had often been in the area before, knew they were seeing a mirage. He presented the bad news to them, sharing the facts as best he could. But insisting their eyes could not deceive them, the students rebelled. Unable to convince them of their error, the professor permitted them to head off in the direction of the "lake," while he would take another course. He made them promise that after they discovered it was a mirage, they would sit down and wait for him to return with help. Three hours later the students arrived at a plush new desert resort which had four swimming pools and six restaurants. Two hours after that they set out in a Land Rover with rangers to search for their teacher. He was never found. (*Therapeutic Metaphors,* META Publications, pp. xi-xii.)

When it comes to marriage and family, you may be like that professor. All that talk of meaningful marriages and happy homes is like a mirage. You may be tired of authors and speakers who promise too much. My friend Marge got tired of dreaming. More than anything else she wanted a husband who would be close to her, who would talk about his emotions, yearn to get her alone at a corner table in a dimly lit restaurant, and passionately desire her. But he remained distant, seemingly not interested in her version of intimacy. When she and her husband became Christians after more than a decade of marriage, her hopes for her marriage soared like those of a new bride.

She read books, took courses, and went to Bible studies, searching for the insights that would turn her marriage around. Titles of books and seminars promised her she could have her pick of a happy, intimate, magnificent, alive, or at least a "maximum" marriage. Pressure on her husband did bring some changes, but they were only temporary. Eventually, he left her. Instead of getting a dynamic marriage, Marge got a divorce.

There are a lot of hurt and disillusioned Marges around. Sometimes we do expect too much. When it comes to our families, most of us are perfectionists. In our minds we carry a picture of the perfect family. Out there somewhere is a home where it's just the way it ought to be. There's a husband who never insults his wife, a wife who never complains, a child who always says, "Yes, Dad, I already took out the garbage." Some authors and speakers reinforce the myth by punctuating their points by stories of such ideal persons.

This book does not guarantee you'll have a fantastic marriage and model children. It is not a guidebook to the trouble-free home. Jesus spoke of building our lives on a solid foundation in His Parable of the Builders. The wise man built his house on a rock, while the foolish one constructed his on sand. Yet the surging streams and strong winds beat against both houses. Building a Christian home, like living a Christian life, is not without some desperate struggles.

Perhaps some of us need to settle for less. We can be too idealistic. One expert put it bluntly: "Three is a crowd: your wife, yourself, and your dream. If you really want to get married, divorce your dream. If you can't build a castle you can at least build a hut, but you'll never be happy in your hut if you're still dreaming of living in a castle" (Michel Quoist, *The Meaning of Success,* Fides Publishers, p. 161).

We gave this book the title *The House on the Rock* to remind us that there are some guidelines for stability in these insecure times. Without creating unrealistic fantasies, we want to cultivate visions of what home life should be. There is some solid real estate still around.

No Vision to Nowhere
Some couples are in danger of having no dreams to work toward or patterns to conform to. They enter marriage without any notion of what it ought to be. Or, if they each do have some picture of married life, they have contrasting ones.

They are like two carpenters building a house, each with a different set of blueprints. Her plans call for intimacy and romance; his design centers on sex, kids, and good meals. He gets all three of these and concludes marriage is awesome; she doesn't get her closeness and thinks marriage is awful. Frustration sets in and then they both give up.

Many couples I know have marriages like the man who told me, "Our marriage was so much boredom. After about five years of it, we sort of said, 'Oh, so this is marriage, ho hum.'" It may be as dangerous to aim for too little as it is to expect too much. Without something to aim for, we can end up investing too little energy into a good marriage, and the relationship slips away from us. Mediocrity can turn into a mess. Just as unrealistic ideals lead to frustration, no ideals at all can lead us nowhere. We stagnate by staying where we are.

Realizing a Dream, Not Stumbling to a Mirage
Most marriages and families can be enriched and enlivened. Many families have found what they aimed for; they consider their homes to be happy and strong. Studies show that one of the qualities of these strong families is commitment. "They were very committed to the family group, as was reflected in the fact that they invested much of their time and energies in it" (Nicholas Stinnett, "Strong Families: A Portrait." *Prevention in Family Services,* David R. Mace (ed.), Sage Publications, p. 32).

One of the major distinctives of the way Christians view the family is that we believe we have some divinely revealed patterns to follow. We are not just to build our homes any way that suits our fancy. God has given us some blueprints for what the family ought to be, as well as instructions for building it.

In the film *Fractured Families,* Ruth Graham, Billy Graham's wife, mentioned how often, as a parent, she was deeply perplexed. "I've needed God's instruction. In many situations that got out of hand, I just had to have wisdom beyond my own."

Wisdom Beyond Our Own
The House on the Rock extracts from the Book of Proverbs its wisdom about marriage and family and relates it to life today. The rewards of following proverbial wisdom are promised in Proverbs. Wisdom is portrayed as a woman who invites you into her house. In her roomy home she has prepared a buffet of homemade delicacies. She calls to those who pass by to enter, eat, and drink. Her guests find that her place is alive and the atmosphere is electric, charged with vitality (Prov. 9:1-6). According to Proverbs, when you follow wisdom, you will "win favor and a good name in the sight of God and man" (3:4). If you walk in the ways of wisdom, they will be pleasant. "All her paths are peace" (3:17). "She is a tree of life to those who embrace her; those

WHEN YOU NEED THE WISDOM OF SOLOMON

who lay hold of her will be blessed" (3:18). Wisdom will keep you from fear (3:24), give safety (3:23), and "yield better returns than gold" (3:14).

On the other hand, the lack of wisdom can lead to tragic consequences. These are graphically depicted by the picture of another woman who also invites guests into her house. As described in Proverbs, the scene is like a TV commercial for a horror movie. A boisterous, bold lady sits beside her house, which is perched on a hill high above the city. From below, the camera fixes on her attractive face as she shouts her invitation: "Come into my house if you need help in making decisions, if you lack insight to cope with life's problems." Then the lens follows the passersby who eagerly push through her open door. Shockingly, the camera zooms onto gray, decaying corpses that litter the dirt floor, open graves spilling over with rotting carcasses.

The woman's name is "Folly." These two women symbolize the basic message of the Book of Proverbs: folly leads to death; wisdom, to life.

Old, Not Outworn

Someone could argue that the proverbs are old and therefore out of date. We need modern answers for contemporary problems, don't we?

I read a sad story in a Manila newspaper when I was in the Philippines. It was about a very poor man who fed and clothed his family by finding and selling scrap metal. One exciting day, while digging for bits and pieces of tanks, jeeps, guns, and bullets deposited in the soil during World War II, he found a large bomb. Anxious for the money the bomb's metal would bring to his needy family, he carted it home. With his tools he began to pry apart the rusting old weapon that had lain in the ground for over twenty years. He was killed when the bomb exploded, blowing up his house and entire family. The bomb's age had not diminished its power.

Proverbs contains a lot of old spiritual blockbusters. They

sometimes look old-fashioned and out-of-date. The names of the proverbs' characters sound odd to modern ears: sluggards, scoundrels, scoffers, and villains. They talk of living on roofs, putting a rod to someone's back, tying stones in slings, catching birds with a snare. Yet, like old buried bombs, they are powerful when put to work. Instead of destruction, they leave healing and life in their path.

The matters proverbs deal with are shockingly relevant. They have a lot to say about anger, for instance. David Mace, a man who has devoted his life to helping families, says that anger is the most critical factor in American marriages today. On another contemporary issue, the place of sex in marriage, Proverbs has a major section. It has more to say about child rearing than any book of the Bible.

Today's experts disagree over all of these issues. Just about everything in the home is bathed in controversy, from how to make love to who should do the dishes. Some tell us to let out our anger, pounding on pillows and screaming in empty rooms. Others maintain that that doesn't control anger; it only generates more of it. Some psychologists say all children need is love; others call for old-fashioned discipline.

A careful study of Proverbs can help us settle for ourselves some of these issues. The reason its writers give for relying on its truth is that wisdom is closely tied to God, like threads in the same shirt. Wisdom is like God because God is truth. Whatever is true is true because it conforms to the nature of God, who is ultimate reality.

When we conform to Proverbs, we are not merely doing things that work. They work and are true because they are a reflection of God the Creator. This is why Proverbs 8:13 states dogmatically: "To fear the Lord is to hate evil." Evil is not merely what is bad for man; it is what is unlike God. On the other hand, good is like God.

Following wisdom is not just a matter of obeying God, as important as that is. Living wisely will result in a fulfilled, enriched life. Wisdom is like the operations manual of a machine. It tells you how to make the gadget work and avoid dumb mistakes that will break or destroy it. Created in God's image, we are to live by God's nature. When a husband is faithful to his wife, he is not just obeying some whim of God; he is being the one-woman man God created him to be. By following Proverbs we discover our true humanity. Being evil is being unlike God and unlike our true selves. Because God is a personal God, He is offended when we are out of step with the created order of things.

How to be at Home with Wisdom

The wisdom of Proverbs is a lot like a nut in a shell. To crack one open, a reader has to understand what a proverb is. Otherwise the proverb is likely to be misunderstood. Take one of the most well known proverbs for an example. Talk to Christian parents about kids who are in trouble and sooner or later someone will mention Proverbs 22:6: "Train a child in the way he should go, and when he is old he will not turn from it." Recently I asked a man about his children. During the long pause before he answered, his head drooped and his eyes shifted back and forth as if he were absentmindedly looking for something he'd lost. He looked beaten, defeated. "Yes, we have children," he finally answered. "I left the ministry because of my son. He's in another state, an alcoholic. Started with a drug problem in Vietnam. My wife had a nervous breakdown over it a number of years ago. That's when I resigned my church. As Christians, we blame ourselves because our son didn't turn out right." When I began to question whether parents are always at fault when their grown children falter, he turned away. Remorse has taken the edge off his life; with the kids gone wrong, nothing will be exactly right again. Many people turn Proverbs 22:6 into a club. Misunderstood proverbs cause a lot of havoc.

I've met people who were angry with God because their marriages or businesses failed even though they had turned them over to God as Proverbs 16:3 told them to do: "Commit to the Lord whatever you do, and your plans will succeed." If we properly interpret these proverbs, they won't lead us to remorse, disappointment, or mistrust of Scripture.

Properly interpret a proverb. Proverbs are a distinct type of literature, just as poetry is. When a colleague of mine and I were teaching a class together, he created a proverb of his own to explain their nature. Waiting for class to begin, he was outside prancing around in an evening drizzle. Glancing down at his shoes, he said, "Aha, I've got it." Smiling before the class, he later gave his example: "Walk in the mud and your shoes will get muddy." He explained. First, a proverb is a brief statement. It packs more of a wallop that way and is more easily memorized. My colleague could have expressed his idea about muddy shoes another way: "Whenever a person commits an act or presents himself to a set of circumstances that is unseemly or in any way tainted with immorality and ungodliness, that person will in some way, no matter how slight, be affected by that influence." This long sentence lulls you to sleep, while the first one about muddy shoes jars you awake.

Proverbs contain carefully arranged words, sometimes in poetic form. The phrases are catchy, easy to say or read. We could say something like, "Your shoes will get muddy if you walk in the mud," but it's less dramatic. We could improve it by making it rhyme: "Walk where its muddy and your shoes will get cruddy." The rhyme seizes attention and aids memory, as in the common English proverb: "A stitch in time saves nine." Rhyme isn't the only way to state things poetically: "Look before you leap" is a kind of poetry, repeating the *L* sound for effect. The Hebrews didn't rhyme words, but they used a variety of poetic effects, especially synthetic parallelism, where different words are used to say the same thing twice. Note the impact of the repetition: "For a man's ways are in full view of the Lord, and He examines all his paths" (5:21).

When the second statement is opposite to the first, the parallelism is called antithetical. The contrast acts as a megaphone, dramatically increasing the force of both lines: "Diligent hands will rule, but laziness ends in slave labor" (12:24).

Another major distinction of proverbs is that they are moral lessons in a package. They get their general message across through the particular, in which it is clothed, as in "A rolling stone gathers no moss." When my fellow teacher spoke of mud, everyone knew he wasn't giving a lesson about clean shoes. He was warning us to stay away from pornography, drugs, bad company, and other negative influences. That's the genius of a proverb: it makes an obvious statement to get across a not-so-obvious truth. In this way, it appeals to the heart as well as the mind; talking of muddy shoes might change a person's attitude toward the movies he watches. Often, things are compared to make a point. Note how the value of truthfulness is emphasized in this comparison: "An honest answer is like a kiss on the lips" (24:26).

The nature of Proverbs is a serious matter when it comes to interpreting them. They can't be interpreted in the same way as statements like "It's raining out" or "We are saved by grace through faith." We must accept the principle a proverb contains without turning it into an ironclad absolute. The Hebrews tended to make general statements without worrying about the exceptions, appealing to the reader's common sense to see this. For example, Proverbs 16:3 assures success to those who first commit their plans to God. But committing alone does not guarantee prosperity; many persons trust God to help them fulfill foolish goals. The proverb is not true for them.

Because they are principles, we must also not turn all of them into promises from God. God is using the wise writers of the proverbs to describe what usually occurs in life. For example, one proverb states, "When a man's ways are pleasing to the Lord, He makes even his enemies live at peace with him" (16:7). The principle here is that being rightly related to God will keep you rightly related to others. God doesn't guarantee this will *always* happen. Jesus was without sin, yet He was murdered by His enemies. To their own detriment parents turn Proverbs 22:6 into a promise: "Train a child in the way he should go, and when he is old he will not turn from it." This proverb is telling us that childhood training is powerful, but it's not telling us it's *always* effective. Some children are too foolish to listen to their parents' teaching. And of course some decide against it in adulthood. In the Old Testament, flagrant rebellion by children was punishable by death (Deut. 21:18-21). They punished the child but we tend to blame the parents.

Also the poetic figures of speech in Proverbs should not be taken literally. For example, Proverbs 6:29 warns that a man who touches another man's wife will not go unpunished. Obviously, the word *touch* is a nice way of talking about having sex with her. Other figures of speech are not so easily identified: hyperbole, for instance, which overstates a matter to make a point. "The Lord tears down the proud man's house but He keeps the widow's boundaries intact" is a way of telling us how God resists the proud and defends the helpless. But obviously there are many proud people in our day whose houses never collapse, literally or figuratively. No doubt the proverbs about debts have such overstatements: "Do not be a man who . . . puts up security for debts; if you lack the means to pay, your very bed will be snatched from under you" (22:26-27). Borrowing was permitted in Old Testament times; the proverb is cautioning a person not to incur indebtedness carelessly.

If we miss the fact that God speaks in many literary forms in the Bible, we may make serious mistakes. In Beaver Valley, Pennsylvania, Bill and Linda Barnhart believed with all their heart that God would heal Justin, their two-year-old son, when he became ill. No doctors were called. Even when his stomach swelled, they continued to believe. After he was listless, pale, and looking like a starving child of a prison camp, they trusted. Eventually they called someone, a funeral director; he called the coroner. Justin's little abdomen contained a four-to-five-pound tumor that had taken all his nourishment, literally starving him to death. The coroner called the police. Found guilty of involuntary manslaughter and endangering the welfare of a child, Bill was fined and sentenced to fifty-nine months probation.

Later, Bill's brother, Bob, was answering a reporter who had asked why medical help was not summoned. He opened his Bible and told the reporter that James 5:16 promises God will save the sick; Jeremiah 46:11 reads: "In vain shalt thou use many medicines; for thou shalt not be cured" (KJV). And then he said, "We feel that God wrote this Bible. Now how are you gonna walk up to the pearly gates when the time comes and say, 'God, You didn't mean Jeremiah 46:11. You didn't mean all these Scriptures.' If He didn't mean it, why did He put it in the Bible?" (Michael E. Ruane, "Jury Renders Guilty Verdict against 'God's Law,'" *Chicago Tribune*, August 20, 1984) Knowing how to find out what the Bible means is an important matter—even one of life and death.

Extract wisdom from your experience. The Scriptures are not our only source of wisdom. From the Book of Proverbs we learn that the wise get wiser from their experiences. This was true of the writers of the proverbs. Unlike prophesies, proverbs are not direct revelations from God given through visions, dreams, or inner conviction. Rather, godly persons learned these truths from observing life. These wise men appeared in Israel around 1000 B.C. They composed and collected these short sayings, which became authoritative Scripture when the Holy Spirit directed their being written in their present form. They consist of insights gleaned from living. Proverbs are like maple syrup. It takes buckets of maple sap to boil into one quart of syrup. Each proverb represents the distillation of a large amount of life.

The writers of Proverbs make it clear we should follow their example and learn from life. Whenever we keep making the same mistakes over and over, it is because we have failed to learn from life. Proverbs 26:11 points out how foolish this is: "As a dog returns to its vomit, so a fool repeats his folly."

The wise person recognizes that both good and bad circumstances are there to teach him because he knows God is behind them. Cartoonist Charles Shultz taught this once through an episode in the life of Charlie Brown. Charlie Brown was carefully building a castle in the beach sand. Standing back to admire his work, he was soon engulfed by a downpour which leveled the castle. Standing before the smooth place where his artwork had once stood, he said: "There must be a lesson here, but I don't know what it is." To grow in Christ, the Christian must look for the message in the misfortune. "The Lord disciplines those He loves, as a father the son he delights in" (3:12).

We should learn from our difficulties. Adversity contains tomorrow's seed corn. "No discipline seems pleasant at the time, but painful. Later on, however, it produces a harvest of righteousness and peace for those who have been trained by it" (Heb. 12:11). God will cause our growth if we respond correctly. Otherwise, He would not be a faithful Father. His correction is not a threat to hurt us; it's a promise to keep us moving ahead. Perhaps studying Proverbs can sharpen our ability to learn from life's hard knocks, not just suffer from them.

The proverbs suggest wisdom is all around us: nature can yield principles for living. "Go to the ant . . . consider its ways and be wise" (6:6). Like the writers of Proverbs we can be like excited explorers, making new discoveries with every new experience. "I applied my heart to what I observed and learned a lesson from what I saw" (24:32). We should also be open to teachers (5:13) and advisers. "A wise man listens to advice" (12:15). Unlike having many cooks spoil a soup, many advisers may lead to success. "Plans fail for lack of counsel, but with many advisers they succeed" (15:22).

Pray for wisdom. Despite all our thinking, reading, asking, and searching, we sometimes stand dumbfounded in front of a desperate problem. Even then Proverbs tells us what to do.

"If you call out for insight and cry aloud for understanding . . . then you will . . . find the knowledge of God. For the Lord gives wisdom" (2:3-6). James refers to this proverb when he urges us to pray for wisdom, telling us that God

"gives generously to all without finding fault" (James 1:5).
A distraught father stood before his kicking and screaming child. He was baffled by his son's temper tantrums. When his son started beating his head against the floor, the father dropped his chin to his chest, shaking his head in a silent prayer, "Help me know what to do." When an idea flashed, he got down on his knees, grabbed his son's head, and said, "Here, let me help you bang it." Careful not to hurt his son, he helped him with his tantrum, instead of resisting it. His surprised son stopped, cured of using tantrums that no longer worked.

Is there always an answer? Is there wisdom for every situation? In a seminar I was conducting, a woman asked this question. Later I learned she had her marriage situation in mind: her husband was a violent man, a compulsive gambler, who hated her and abused her daughter. Enduring this situation for more than a decade, she was convinced it defied resolution. Yet I told her, "God has wisdom to match any situation." Wisdom might not tell her how to change her husband; it might indicate she should stop trying. To spare her daughter and herself from harm, she might eventually have to separate from him until the consequences of his irresponsible actions motivated him to change. I am convinced that God will lead to wisdom all those who ask for it.

Apparently, God doesn't always answer the prayer by miraculously inserting ideas into our heads like typing words onto a computer screen. Right after He commands us to pray, He urges us to do something else (2:3-4).

Search for wisdom. Wisdom is so priceless that the search for it is compared to the hunt for hidden treasure (2:4). In the summer of 1985, we were awestruck by the reports of deep-sea divers when they came upon the treasure of the sunken Spanish galleon *Nuestra Senora de Atocha.* The bars of silver, they said, were "stacked up like cordwood as far as the eye can see." While millions envied, Mel Fisher and his crew began to haul to the surface gold and silver worth $400 million. During the salvaging they reported "recovering emeralds by the quart." The estimated value of all the treasure was $4 billion.

Those of us who thrill over finding such a fortune might not be so excited about searching for it. It's one thing to covet what Fisher found; it's another to pay the price of his search. Fisher began his quest in 1970. In the fifteen years of meticulously criss-crossing the area of the sunken ship, he found and spent $70 million. When money was scarce, his divers went without pay, sometimes for as long as six years. His ships were outfitted with side scanning sonar, the most advanced underwater detection machinery available. The hunt cost him the lives of his son and daughter-in-law when their ship, the *Northwest,* capsized in a storm. No wonder Fisher, a former chicken farmer, once quipped that hunting for treasure was not as easy as a "chicken picking corn" (Francis Norris, "$400 Million Treasure: A Record Find off Key West," *Motor Boating and Sailing,* vol. 1, 156. October, 1985, pp. 48-50, 110; "Spanish Wreck Bursting with Emeralds," *Chicago Tribune*, May 29, 1986).

Are we that committed to the search for wisdom? Do Christian husbands work that hard to find out how to love their wives? Do parents put that kind of effort into learning how to discipline their children? Do we Christians really struggle that much to conquer a bad temper, learn how to stop nagging, control our gossiping, or learn how to handle a rebellious teenager? "If you look for it [wisdom] as for silver and search for it as for hidden treasure, then you will understand the fear of the Lord and find the knowledge of God" (2:4-5).

Knowing Not Equal to Growing
But having the answer is still not all the answer. The man sitting before me knew this too well. He and I were talking about his problems managing his children. Everything I suggested he already knew about, being an intelligent man who had been to several counselors and read books about child

rearing. At one point in our conversation, he suddenly closed his eyes and became silent for a few minutes. Then he shook his head back and forth and said, "I know I should discipline my children; but why don't I do it?" All of us have asked this type of question. We are well aware of the fact that knowing does not always lead to doing. In the next chapter, using Proverbs as a guide, we will deal with this matter of how to change.

Chapter
TWO

FROM HEAD TO HEART TO HABIT

Pay attention to the sayings of the wise.
PROVERBS 22:17

"When my teenage daughter asks, 'Dad, may I go out tonight?' I put my education to work," the superintendent of our local high school told me. "First, I sift through all the adolescent psychology courses I've had, then the secondary education classes. Finally, my mind runs through the management courses of my Ph.D. program. Then I confidently tell her, 'Go ask your mother.'"

It's difficult to get what we know behind the front doorways of our homes. Yet wisdom is not really wisdom unless it's practiced. This is a hard concept for us modern people to grasp, because we tend to separate knowledge from behavior.

Putting the "Is" into Wisdom

For the Hebrews, wisdom included action. This point is made in the opening verses of Proverbs. Wisdom is called by many names: "knowledge," "discretion," "guidance," and "insight." But wisdom also consists in "doing what is right and just and fair" (1:3). A person is not counted wise when he only *knows* what is just, fair, and right. He is wise when he *is* just, fair, and right.

We Christians sometimes kid ourselves into thinking that simply learning more of the Bible will automatically lead to change. In the early years of my Christian life, I so often thought I had conquered a problem when I hadn't. Hearing a sermon on worrying, I left the church thinking my worrying days were over. I soon learned that knowing does not amount to growing, even when what I knew was in the Bible. James makes it clear that it is possible to know truth without practicing it. "Anyone, then, who knows the good he ought to do and doesn't do it, sins" (4:17).

It makes a lot of sense to include action in wisdom. An ex-Navy man told us how the Navy showed him that knowledge isn't worth much unless it's put to work. In his basic training, he was taught by lecture and films how to handle himself in an emergency. Following weeks of instruction, he and his other classmates were taken to a lake where they went on board a strange-looking vessel. They found themselves in a small room on the lower deck awaiting further orders. Chatting and drinking Cokes, they were alarmed when the door flew open, followed by a torrent of water crashing down the stairs. Unable to get out, they stood, helplessly waiting for someone to rescue them. When waist high, the water stopped; then it slowly receded. They were spared from drowning, but not from a dressing-down, which came shortly afterward.

An irate officer told them they had failed the test. The room contained all they needed to close the door and block the water. But, in this simulated emergency, they had failed to act as they had been taught. It wouldn't be hard to argue that they really did not know what to do in an emergency, even though before the simulated shipwreck, they could have passed a written test on the subject.

No Tough Place Like Home
While we all know that it's a giant step from precept to practice, why is it usually such a difficult thing to change the

way we act in our homes? For one thing, many of us were ill-prepared for family living. We're like baseball players in a major league game without good minor league experience. We carry into our own marriages the troubles and inadequacies of our childhood homes. If our parents weren't very close to each other, being intimate may be hard for us. We'll probably have a hard time handling conflict if our parents fought a lot. If we weren't disciplined correctly, it will be harder for us to train our children. Research confirms that the childhood family has a powerful influence on us. The patterns of the past sometimes clash with the demands of the present.

People may object to this, saying, "I don't imitate my parents; I try hard not to be like them." Yet, such persons are still affected by their parents. Instead of following their parents' example, they are reacting to it. A girl whose parents divorced may not have the same lack of commitment to her marriage as her parents. She may take her marriage so seriously that she causes trouble by demanding too much of herself and her husband. So much of the time we are either acting like our parents or reacting against them. The Book of Proverbs doesn't put a lot of emphasis on analyzing our pasts. Though it recognizes the powerful influence others have on us, it puts the stress on changing our present behavior. The past cannot be used as an excuse for our present failings, but understanding our pasts can help us explain the present. It can shed light on why we have certain struggles and teach us patience in dealing with them.

The wise men of Proverbs promise both wisdom and discipline (1:2). Contained in their sayings are principles for bringing about change in our lives.

When Knowledge Takes Second Place
Surprisingly, acquiring wisdom is not the first step toward change, according to the Book of Proverbs. This is strangely different from what we find elsewhere. To fly a plane, build a

house, or cook a meal, you need knowledge first. Yet, Proverbs says bluntly, "The fear of the Lord is the beginning of knowledge" (1:7). Fearing God doesn't always mean being afraid, but it does mean being awestruck, reverencing Him as the Supreme Being. To fear God is to recognize His sovereignty over all. It is equivalent to what we mean by conversion. The person who has an awesome respect for God's place in his life has a basis for righteous life. This makes it a sort of first principle of wisdom. For unless a person has the person of God as his Lord, he is in a position neither to know nor to do what is right.

Proverbs helps us acquire a "disciplined and prudent life, [to do] what is right and just and fair" (1:3). A person who uses knowledge for evil is not called wise, but crafty and shrewd. In Scripture, wisdom is the blending of the intellectual, the spiritual, and the moral. "The fear of the Lord is the beginning of knowledge, but fools despise wisdom and discipline" (1:7). The smart person is the moral one, and the moral person is one who has a reverence for God. In this light, the meaning of the well-known passage Proverbs 3:5-6 is clear: "Trust in the Lord with all your heart and lean not on your own understanding; in all your ways acknowledge Him, and He will make your paths straight." To lean not on your own understanding shows a willingness to pit God's truth against your own opinion: "Do not be wise in your own eyes; fear the Lord and shun evil" (3:7).

Humble Pie Is Nutritious

A second key to growing is to be open to new ideas and solutions. To be wise, we must be humble. "With humility comes wisdom" (11:2). Pride slams the door on wisdom. "The way of a fool seems right to him, but a wise man listens to advice" (12:15). Being wise in his own eyes, the proud person feels no need to listen. Wisdom says, "I hate pride and arrogance" (8:13). The wise person is open to the advice of parents, friends, and others in a search for the will of God.

Christians improve their lives as athletes improve their performance. After a game, a football player must listen to his coaches and watch films that brutally show his mistakes. Humility and honesty make him open to receive correction. Like the athlete, the Christian should be open to rebuke from God and correction from others.

Receiving rebuke may be the most painful part of growing, but it may also be the most crucial. According to Proverbs 15:31, "He who listens to a life-giving rebuke will be at home with the wise." Teachers admire a humble student. The level of intelligence and discipline matter little if the pupil isn't teachable. Otherwise, he or she won't respond to the comments in the margin of the paper or the corrections on the exam. A prominent educator of the early twentieth century, George Coe, told how he loved this kind of student. At times, he chose to be ruthless in his critique of a student's work. When the scholar came to his office to complain, Coe told him to feel honored. "I was frank with you because I knew you could bounce," he said. For Coe, bouncing back was the stuff of personal growth. Apparently, our ability to "bounce" matters a great deal to God, who gives grace to the humble (3:34). There is no welcome mat for wisdom at the door of the proud person's heart. To that person, wisdom says: "If you had responded to my rebuke, I would have poured out my heart to you and made my thoughts known to you" (1:23).

Cultivate a Distaste for Foolishness

A third guideline for growing is to avoid foolishness. One of the major features of the Book of Proverbs is its elaborate description of fools. The writers of wisdom were not just writing *about* fools; they were writing *to* them. Fools were people outside the sphere of godliness. Today we would call them unregenerate persons who had not accepted Christ as Saviour. The wisdom teacher's message to fools was to stop rejecting God and His wisdom (1:14-27).

This constant reference to foolishness is also meant, at least in part, for us to see the bad side of ourselves and our behavior. All of us are capable of being fools or acting foolishly. By regularly reading Proverbs, we can develop a greater disgust with our inappropriate behavior. A person who is a poor listener, for example, may be goaded to improve by Proverbs 18:13: "He who answers before listening—that is his folly and his shame." To take another example, think of the effect Proverbs 29:11 might have on someone who is hot tempered: "A fool gives full vent to his anger, but a wise man keeps himself under control." The Proverbs are giving us concrete snapshots of people who habitually do these things to warn us against doing the same.

Proverbs' Fools Are Not Clowns
Fools stand in stark contrast to the wise. Fools are not retarded persons or funny clowns. The proverb that warns us to stay away from fools isn't forbidding contact with the retarded, uneducated, or mentally ill. Fools are people who not only lack wisdom, but avoid it as if it were a disease.

There are several kinds of fools in Proverbs. Distinguishing one from the other will help us better understand individual proverbs. For example, one proverb tells us that a person without judgment (a fool) can learn from punishment (10:13), while another says a fool rejects his father's discipline (15:5). Each is a different type of fool. Five of them are prominent in Proverbs.

Peti. This fool is called "simple." The major trait of the *peti* is that he or she is easily influenced. Apt to believe anything he hears, this fool needs reliable teachers (14:15).

Hasar leb. Usually this fool is referred to as "lacking sense." He or she lacks experience and the good sense that comes from seeing the outcome of doing the wrong thing. If a young person, this kind of fool can be helped by spanking and other kinds of corrective measures. Since they don't recognize the consequencs of their actions, they need to learn from experience, not just from verbal instructions. Life's hardships may eventually make this kind of fool wise (10:13).

Kesil. Simply translated "fool," this word refers to the person who hates knowledge (1:22) and has nothing to do with God (1:29). This person is very self-centered (18:2) and has no remorse for the wrong he or she does (10:23).

Ewil. This word is another one that is translated "fool." It refers to a person who is quite morally corrupt. The corruption is such that if the person were ground with grain, the folly would not be removed (27:22). This person is argumentative; in fact, if a woman, she is said to destroy her marriage with her words (14:1).

Les. Translated with the word "scoffer," this fool is so incorrigible that other people detest him (24:9). Pride underlies his or her compulsion to mock everything and everyone (21:24), including God.

A Hope-Fool Outlook

We've got to keep some things in mind if we are to benefit fully from this tour of Proverbs' gallery of fools. First, even the worst of them is not beyond help. They picture the depravity of the human heart without God. Paul the Apostle uses the description of fools to depict the condition of all persons under sin, quoting from Psalm 14 (Rom. 3:11-13). Christ can change the heart of the most depraved. These portraits underscore how hopeless life is without Christ.

Second, this gallery can help us identify fools, but we should be careful of pinning labels on people. Young persons especially might be hurt by our negative judgments. I remember how hard some of us tried to convince a mother to stop calling her child evil. He was doing a good job of acting out the image she had of him. Granted, Proverbs do urge us to recognize a fool when we see one, because they sometimes deserve special treatment. We must protect the *peti* from bad influence and concentrate on teaching him.

FROM HEAD TO HEART TO HABIT

However, if we try correcting a *les,* the scoffer, he'll return it with hatred (Prov. 9:8). Those of us who deal with troubled persons today know they can't always be treated in normal ways. Pleas and rebukes are often wasted on alcoholics, compulsive gamblers, delinquent teens, criminals, and others. Any response is a wrong one with some people. Perhaps this is what two contradictory proverbs are telling us. One counsels "Answer a fool according to his folly, or you'll make him wise in his own eyes" (26:5). The other advises us: "Do not answer a fool according to his folly, or you will be like him yourself" (26:4). Some people put you in a no-win situation. Not that we can't do something with fools, even if it's only prayerfully standing by while their hitting bottom gets a message through to them.

Third, this gallery of persons is more a moral and spiritual picture than it is a psychological one. The Book of Proverbs doesn't deal with all of life; we know that mental, physical, and emotional illness can cause people to behave like fools. Alcoholism and depression are among the problems that may have physical causes. We should try to understand any troubled child or spouse before concluding theirs is only a moral problem. If we are wise, we will learn from our experience and scientific research. We must avoid too swiftly labeling someone a fool instead of loving him or her as a person. (To do a more complete study of each of these kinds of fools, consult these verses. *Peti:* 1:22; 1:32; 21:11. *Hasar leb:* 10:13; 11:12; 15:21; 24:30-31. *Kesil:* 1:22; 1:32; 10:23; 13:2; 17:24; 29:11. *Ewil:* 10:10; 14:1; 20:3; 27:22. *Les:* 1:22; 3:34; 13:1; 21:24; 22:10; 24:9; 29:20.)

Maturity at Heart
One of the most important guidelines for growth in Proverbs is that we get truth into our hearts. "Apply to your heart what I teach, for it is pleasing when you keep [wise sayings] in your heart" (22:17-18). *Heart* in the Old Testament refers to the interior of the person: it includes the mind but is more

than the mind, referring as well to the will and affections. To have God's truth in the heart means to have it change our values and transform our desires. By constantly reading, studying, and memorizing Scripture, we can inject it into our inner selves. Pouring over God's truth is like storing food in a cellar. Not only is it available when we need it, but like apples in a storehouse, its odor can permeate the interior of our souls. A person may not even be conscious of how Scripture about the dangers of anger may be mellowing his or her bad temper. A woman with a negative attitude toward sex might find herself slowly changed by the biblical truth she has learned about love. Taken to heart, Scripture might make a grouchy person more cheerful, a lazy one more ambitious, an unfaithful one more dependable.

Besides memorizing Scripture, we can get it into our hearts by meditating on it. Though the term *meditation* is not found in Proverbs, the book constantly encourages us to keep God's commands in our hearts and not forget them (3:1). To meditate means to recall Scripture and ponder how it will apply to a given situation.

For a Change of Face

Continually having God's Word in front of our inner eyes will create positive images of what we ought to be, which will in turn eventually make us into their likeness. Nathaniel Hawthorne's short story "The Old Stone Face" is a remarkable picture of this process. The tale centers on Earnest, a young boy who longs to see the legend of the stone face fulfilled. Sitting on their back porch, his parents explained how one day a great man would come to their village who would resemble the figure on the mountain that towered over their village. Earnest could see the face that nature had playfully carved in the mountain behind his home. No sculptor had chiseled it, but it was clearly there; the high forehead, the prominent nose, the pleasant smile, and firm chin.

Earnest's yearning to see in the flesh the person he saw on

the mountain was like a pain inside of him. Whenever the rumor spread that the great man had been located, he was among the first to find out if it was so. It never was. During Earnest's teen years, there was General Blood and Thunder. But his face, hardened and cruel from years of battle and killing, was unlike the kind expression Earnest saw in the old stone face. Others came and went. Though in his lifetime the strong face had not come, Earnest had longingly studied it, noting the humility mixed with strength, the love mingled with steadfastness of purpose.

By the time he was an old man, Earnest had built quite a reputation for himself. His loving service to his community had won him acclaim; his wisdom and maturity made others seek him out for help and counsel. One day an old poet visited the village just to bask in the splendor of this man, Earnest. After warm, animated conversation, the two old men walked slowly to the village park, where Earnest would give his usual Sunday evening lecture. The poet sat in front staring at Earnest as the old man began his speech. The setting sun lit up the marvelous stone face behind Earnest. Glancing from Earnest's face to the stone face and back again and again, the poet shifted and bounced in excitement. Unable to constrain himself, he interrupted Earnest's speech, shouting, "Earnest, he is the stone face. Earnest, he is the stone face." The astonished crowd confirmed the discovery. But on the way home, Earnest violently denied that he could be the mythical one.

Whether he was or not didn't matter; Hawthorne had made his point. The many years of looking at the stone face had slowly changed Earnest into the image he saw. His vision formed his values and desires, which shaped his behavior. Paul described this process: "And we, who with unveiled faces all reflect [or *contemplate*] the Lord's glory, are being transformed into His likeness with ever-increasing glory, which comes from the Lord, who is the Spirit" (2 Cor. 3:18). Jesus Christ is the glory of God; continuous communion with Him will make us more and more like Him.

Turning Yourself Inside Out

Our own image of self affects our behavior. A best-selling book by Maxwell Maltz, a plastic surgeon, explains how he learned this. He tells of removing the bandages from a patient after he had performed surgery to reconstruct her face. When he saw how attractive she looked, he marveled over what his hands and modern medicine could accomplish. But when the patient looked into the mirror he handed her, she sighed in resignation and said, "I knew it would never work." Though outwardly she was now pretty, inwardly she still felt ugly. Unless she changed her attitude, the surgery would do little for her self-confidence. The surgeon had seen this same kind of thing before; he had straightened a man's lame arm and hand, only to see the man continue to hold the new limb by his side, unused as before the operation. This led the doctor into experimenting with how to get people to change on the inside according to the changes he had made on the outside. His book, called *Psycho-Cybernetics,* explains how we can change ourselves if we will change our inner image. We can achieve success if we think success. There is a solid biblical truth here. What we believe we are and ought to be will do a great deal to shape what we become.

Faith It

All this concentration on what we ought to be could generate a lot of guilt and frustration. Another guideline from Proverbs can help prevent that. We are to recognize that only God can change us. God's action occurs in our activity. "In his heart a man plans his course, but the Lord determines his steps" (Prov. 16:9). God is sovereign over all, according to these proverbs: no matter what happens, God "works out everything for His own ends" (16:4). Therefore Proverbs tells us to trust God (22:19). Our abilities are limited. Without His power and guidance, we would go astray.

One of my favorite sports stories powerfully makes this point. The mother of a small child, Walter, heard the doctors say, "Your son will never walk again." But she would not give in to the infantile paralysis that had damaged her son. With determination, she massaged his legs, soaking them in hot compresses until finally he was able to walk and even run. One day after watching boys compete in the high jump at a high school track meet, Walter said to himself, *I want to become the world champion high jumper.*

Later, he competed in high school and then college. Once when returning home after hours of painful practice, his wife said to him, "Walter, you not only have strength in your legs; you have it in your heart." Together, they coined a phrase: "the strength of belief." Any accomplishment requires the confidence that it can be done. One day in an indoor track meet, Walter cleared the bar at six feet eleven and one half inches. When the official placed the bar at six feet eleven and five eighths inches, the crowd recognized that it represented a new world record. On the first try Walter tipped the bar and it fell to the ground with him. It was the same on the second try. As he stood back for his third and final attempt, Walter thought of the phrase, "the strength of belief." Picturing himself going over the bar as he ran, he then jumped; the boy they thought would never walk became the world high jump champion, Walter Davis. Davis had faith in faith. Much more, our faith is in God. The control of our tempers, our sensuality, our speech, and our sinful natures is possible because of Him. We do not change simply because we know truth, but because we know and depend on God.

Plotting and Plodding
Yet we must be careful not to think that growing in faith is effortless. Trust is not a substitute for hard work. Work puts action to our faith: faith puts confidence in our action.

As a counselor, teacher, and pastor, I have often seen people use faith as an excuse for doing nothing. Husbands fail to do anything about their crumbling marriages because they somehow think God will work it out. Parents pray for a teenager on drugs, afraid to face the problem and seek help.

Though sometimes we can do nothing but pray, most situations call for action on our part. Proverbs 21:31 shows how faith and action are combined: "The horse is made ready for the day of battle, but victory rests with the Lord."

Proverbs stresses the crucial role human planning and effort play in maturing. We are told to plan for good: "But those who plan what is good find love and faithfulness" (14:22). "The wisdom of the prudent is to give thought to their ways" (14:8).

We could improve our family life by making a list of areas that need to be renewed, then numbering them according to priority, asking which hurts the most and which will cause the most trouble if neglected. Then we can choose the most crucial problem and devise a scheme for dealing with it.

If it's a skill we need to learn or an attitude we need to cultivate, we may need to practice, practice, practice. Frequently, I've seen a certain colleague behaving strangely in the hallway outside my office. But those of us who see him swinging his empty fists in a circle around his body know that he is simply practicing his golf swing. If a husband, for example, gave the same kind of effort to learning to affirm his wife, he would soon make it a habit.

Keep Company with Giants

Besides our plans and our struggles, God will use other people to help us change. "He who walks with the wise grows wise, but a companion of fools suffers harm" (13:20). "As iron sharpens iron, so one man sharpens another" (27:17). "Do not make friends with a hot-tempered man, do not associate with one easily angered, or you may learn his ways and get yourself ensnared" (22:24-25). Sometimes we avoid people who are stronger and more mature than ourselves because we want to stay comfortable in our immaturity. But we shouldn't be afraid to walk with giants. Meeting regularly in a growth group where there is honesty, encouragement, and challenge can be one of the most effective means of remodeling our lives and enriching our marriages.

Share Your Care

Sometimes we need to confide in someone about our struggles. Counseling is not a modern invention. One proverb suggests that another person may help us think through our own thoughts. "The purposes of a man's heart are deep waters, but a man of understanding draws them out" (20:5). One scholar insists that this refers "to counseling or drawing out the deepest thoughts from inside a person for therapeutic reasons." Some thoughts need to be brought to the surface where they can be examined and dealt with (Robert Alden, *Proverbs,* Baker Book House, p. 149).

Our sinful nature backs away from problems, wanting only to escape and forget. The wise person faces them. Malcomb Jones learned this in a dramatic way. Having crashed in a small plane in the Florida Everglades, he saw that his unconscious friend was bleeding badly. Knowing he would have to go for help, he started wading through the swamps toward the nearest town. Soon, in water above his waist, he came upon a huge pair of eyes, glowing in the moonlight. Beside them on each side were smaller ones, indicating that he was before an alligator nest. First to occupy his mind were the words of the old-timers in the region: "Never walk into a nest of alligators." Then came the words, "I am with you always." With confidence in God's presence, he sloshed straight ahead, saying, "Mama alligator, I don't want to hurt you or your kids, but I have to get help for my friend. Here I come." In response, the huge alligator clapped her jaws, tail slashing in the water, and slithered off to the side, all the little pairs of eyes following. Later telling his story, Jones said that he must have stomped headlong through a dozen nests. During the long night, he said, he learned a great lesson: "To always face my problems head on."

Chapter
THREE

WHAT *COMMIT* MEANT

The covenant...made before God.
PROVERBS 2:17

Once there was a satisfied married pair who jogged along happily in their marriage until someone talked them into a "romantic weekend." Until then, they were doing fine: they shared interest in the kids, the house, the husband's job, and so on. But when they packed their bags and headed off to be "intimate," their troubles began. A Christian author, Mary Pride, explains what happened: "On the way to their resort, they began to talk about 'us' rather than their common interests, as they had always done before. After only one day they returned, shocked to discover that when it came to talking about 'us' they had nothing to say" (*The Way Home*, Crossway Books, p. 18). Soon after they were divorced.

Their problem, according to Mary Pride, was not that they couldn't be intimate; their mistake was that they even tried. They had a perfectly good marriage until someone happened along to raise their expectations.

> Intimate marriage isn't biblical. Intimate marriage demands that marriage be self-centered. It insists that kicks and thrills are the reasons for marriage. It tries to squash everyone into one mold—that of hedonistic teenagers—and destroys all who can't fit. (Pride, p. 18)

An Easy Answer to Marital Dissatisfaction

Mary Pride's answer to the divorce problem is simple enough: don't expect so much from marriage. In fact, don't expect anything; that's selfish. Realize we have died with Christ and that everything is for Him. Marriage is a place of service to God. Raise kids and be good Christian brothers and sisters to each other. Try to make more of it, and disillusionment will set in and you'll want out. Here's a unique solution to the contemporary divorce problem. Expect little and you'll not be disappointed. Be like the man who tried to be an expert archer; he got so frustrated trying to hit the center of the target that he finally shot an arrow into the barn and then drew a target around it: *bull's-eye.* Hanging on to impossible goals leads to dashed hopes. To avoid nightmares, stop dreaming.

According to Mary Pride, the couple that traipsed off for a weekend alone were asking for it. They could not be expected to fill up forty hours with just each other—without the kids to fuss over, the dishes to wash, the budget to balance, what were they to do? They had a biblical marriage. This "attempt to turn a perfectly good marriage into an intimate marriage has led to many, many divorces" (p. 18).

Marriage: A Channel of Blessing or Just a Rut?

Mary Pride has written about a critical issue. Exactly what is marriage to be? Does the Bible suggest that making too much of marriage tempts people to divorce? Should we shoot down our ideals before they shoot down our marriages? Let's begin answering this by looking at one of the most prominent verses in the Bible about marriage:

> He who finds a wife finds what is good and receives favor from the Lord. (Prov. 18:22)

Though the word *marriage* never occurs in Proverbs, marriage is very visible. The Hebrews used other terms to refer to it—most often the words *husband* and *wife,* as in this proverb. It affirms the bliss, the goodness, of the married state. Ancient versions of this verse added *good* to the word *wife,* but the original did not. It's not that it's great to have a good wife: it's great simply to have a wife. And the benefit is special; it is an excellence from God. The man "receives favor from the Lord" (18:22). Marriage is one of the special channels through which God sends His blessing. The proverb does not tell us why marriage is good. It could be referring merely to the fact that a wife can cook his meals and bear his children. But the marriage treasure contains more than that. "Be captivated" by your wife's love, advises another proverb. "May her breasts satisfy you always" (5:19). Within marriage people discover love. Its special quality appears early in the Hebrew story: "Isaac brought her into the tent of his mother Sarah, and he married Rebekah. So she became his wife, and he loved her; and Isaac was comforted after his mother's death" (Gen. 24:67).

That God is behind the scene of a good marriage is the emphasis of Proverbs 19:14: "Houses and wealth are inherited from parents, but a prudent wife is from the Lord."

This sounds much like James' words: "Every good and perfect gift is from above, coming down from the Father" (1:17). The Apostle Paul specifically identifies marriage as one of those gifts. In writing of marriage and singleness he writes, "Each man has his own gift from God; one has this gift, another has that" (1 Cor. 7:7).

Marriage has been created by God "to be received with thanksgiving by those who believe and know the truth. For everything God created is good, and nothing is to be rejected if it is received with thanksgiving" (1 Tim. 4:3-4).

It will do a lot for our marriages if we recognize what a great "prize" we are to one another. "A wife of noble character who can find? She is worth far more than rubies" (Prov. 31:10). "A wife of noble character is her husband's crown" (12:4). When married, your attitudes and behavior and accomplishments are not for yourself and your reputation alone: you and what you are add luster to your partner's life. We are important to each other—worth more than treasure and rubies. We are each God's gift to the other.

Who Needs Marriage?
For various reasons, Christians sometimes downplay the value of marriage. Sometimes this is caused by an inadequate view of our needs. Knowing Christ as Saviour is supposed to alleviate human deficiencies. Lawrence Crabb has made this idea the foundation of his book *The Marriage Builder* (Zondervan). Though his book is loaded with insight, I believe it is wrong when it asserts: "I am instructed by God to believe that my needs are already met, and therefore I am to live selflessly, concerned only with the needs of others" (p. 21). Mary Pride comes to a similar conclusion, only from a negative point of view. Because "we deny ourselves and take up our cross," we are therefore free from the idea that "marriage is for me," or even for "us" (pp. 19–20). These authors are trying to liberate people from being upset when their partners are not measuring up. Seeing that our needs are already met in Christ is a means of defusing that anger.

Biblically and practically, this is the wrong way to handle marital dissatisfaction. Knowing Christ as Saviour does not satisfy what marriage is designed for. Though we receive love, acceptance, intimacy, significance, and more from God, we still need others to love us and make us feel important. God is not a substitute for human companionship any more than He is a substitute for lunch. When Paul writes, "My God will meet all your needs" (Phil. 4:19), it is a promise that He will do so, not a statement that He has. And when there is a shortage in an area, He will enable us to endure and be content until He provides. In the meantime, we suffer. A Christian, like any other person, needs fellowship with others to be emotionally healthy. If he or she doesn't get it in marriage, it would be wise to seek friendship with others of the same sex and not merely think no social need exists.

Granted Crabb is correct in saying that at times we try to have our spouses meet needs that only God can meet. A wife should not look to her husband for ultimate security, for example. Putting another person in the place of God is a form of idolatry. But the woman can still expect a relative amount of security from a diligent husband. A woman who is married to an undependable man is bound to have bouts of discouragement and feelings of insecurity. Protestant reformer John Calvin did not spiritualize away the pain of enduring personal need. In his commentary on 1 Peter, he writes: "The faithful are not logs of wood, nor have they so divested themselves of human feelings, but that they are affected with sorrow, fear danger and feel poverty as an evil, and persecutions as hard and difficult to be borne" (*Commentaries on the Catholic Epistles,* translated and edited by John Owen, Calvin Translation Society, p. 32).

There are also some practical problems with the view that all the Christian's needs are met. If all our needs are met in Christ, or if all our needs are crucified with Christ, it makes a person feel selfish if he enjoys marriage. There is nothing wrong with thinking that "marriage is for me" or for "us," as Mary Pride seems to think. To enjoy God's gifts does not betray Him, as long as my first allegiance is to Him. There is no need to feel guilty about enjoying sex, being with friends, or eating a good meal.

The most troubling thing about this view is that it can reduce the sense of the urgency of meeting other people's needs. Isn't it somewhat contradictory to say as Crabb does that a person is instructed to live as if all his needs have been met in Christ and then to go about unselfishly meeting the needs of others? If other people have Christ, why the rush to meet their needs? I think this attitude of individualism creates problems in marriage and the church. We expect Christ to meet people's needs and fail to realize how desperate they are. We become insensitive, especially in areas where we ourselves have no problems. A man, for example, who has little need for intimate conversation with his wife, merely because he has the temperament of a loner, may think his low need for companionship is really because he is so spiritual. He may judge his wife's high need for companionship as a symptom of a low level of spirituality. To be fair to Crabb, he does make it clear that we should not ignore each other's needs. But his view could dull a person's sensitivity.

Assessing Our Net Worth

Pondering our worth to our lover should definitely increase our own self-esteem. Serving God includes serving my spouse. Living for my spouse's welfare is not competing with living for God's glory. Only if loyalty to my spouse causes me to reject God does it become wrong. But if I do not fail to love God, I cannot love my spouse too much. Measure a husband's affection, says Paul, by what it took for Christ to hang by nails from a piece of wood (Eph. 5:25).

It's easy to bypass the home when we think of glorifying God. Men who neglect the bedroom for the church boardroom are often highly praised for their dedication. We acclaim women who rush from one Bible study to another, getting the time and energy it takes by shortchanging their husbands. We slave to prove our value outside the home often because we overlook our worth within it. This can be done in the name of God or greed.

This was the theme of a recent TV show. A professional football player's sense of self-worth was threatened by the loss of his position on the team. When a rookie was close to replacing him, he became unglued. Focusing on his fading fame and his shattered sense of self-esteem, he lashed out in anger at his wife and child when they tried to comfort him. His ego began to mend when his wife countered his outrage. "When you are no longer important to your fans, you will still be important to me." In time, this thought penetrated his depression. Our value to our spouses should foster a sense of dignity. We may not be jewels or treasures to many people in this world, but we are God's priceless gifts to our marriage partners.

In today's scheme of things, it's not easy to cling to this idea. Being a "crown" to a husband is nothing like being vice president. Being a husband can't compare to being a surgeon. If self-esteem, respect, or worth were measured in pounds, how many ounces would being a husband, wife, father, or mother weigh? In Proverbs the noble wife was a respected person: "Give her the reward she has earned, and let her works bring her praise at the city gate" (31:31). This doesn't mean we look down on service outside the home, but that we exalt service within it. Our roles of executive secretary, salesman of the year, and union carpenter too easily eclipse the roles of husband and wife. Then we resent the demands of spouse and children because they interfere with this greater glory. We become impatient, shabby partners and parents in our striving to make our mark, all the while excusing ourselves by our list of items we call priorities.

While writing this book, I had a bout with this disease. Resentment, discontent, and anger are the major symptoms. I resented the time I was still investing in my children, was angry because they still depended on me, and discontented over their sapping energy from me which I could devote to authoring "great" books. To my wife, Ginger, I groaned, "I am tired of being a parent; we've been at it for the last thirty years." After numerous repairs of my college son's car and dishing out money for another who had an employment problem, I came down with a good case of self-pity. My wife listened in silence; the Lord with patience (I trust). Then in more sober moments, when walking the dog and bewailing my plight, my subconscious got a message to me. It reminded me that being a provider for one's children is one of the greatest responsibilities a person has, that being a good father to four children is a glorious privilege. This is not a lesser role. On the world's stage, maybe. But not in God's theater. He has handed me a major part in the play He has written and produced. I need to stay with it and play it for all its worth. "Break a leg," I cheered myself. "Go out there and give it all you have." I was cured—for the time being.

The Book of Proverbs describes the distractions and hindrances that can destroy our homes if we are careless and flippant about them. If we don't do our best to make it fall together, it may fall apart. Marriage is like the old joke about the man who was leaning against the wall. When he said he was holding it up, people laughed. When he stepped away, the wall crashed. Marriage needs to be held up. A couple doesn't just make a marriage on their wedding day; they make it every day after. Love is not an eternal flame; it needs fuel or it dies.

Forces within and without threaten our relationships. Some marriages cave in even though the outer shell remains. "My husband and I never talk anymore," a Christian woman said to me. Her face showed no particular emotion. She was like a kerosene lamp after the flame had gone out. I detected no flicker as she continued. "We haven't had sex for more than a year." Her middle-aged husband was a deacon in the church, heavily involved in ministry. "Don't you want to revive what you once had?" I asked. In the next moment I knew why she had emotionally flamed out. "It's just not worth it. My husband doesn't care about me. He never shares anything intimate. Women in his church music group tell me things he is thinking and feeling that I never hear from him." She confessed to almost having had an affair a few years before; she wasn't sure it would happen again, but she said she didn't care if it did. But she *should* care about the threat of an affair and the vitality of her marriage.

"Unfaith-Fool"
Proverbs underscores how serious unfaithfulness is. The strongest statement about marital ties is found in a surprising place—in a proverb about an adulteress. The wayward wife is described as one who has "left the partner of her youth and ignored the covenant she made before God" (2:17). Two broken things lie in her past, like shattered pieces of priceless porcelain: a friendship forsaken and a promise ignored.

The truth in this verse reveals why the Book of Proverbs comes down so hard on those who don't remain true blue.

The man who embraces another man's wife is a man whose "evil deeds . . . ensnare him," the "cords of his sin" holding him fast (5:22). Eventually "he will die for lack of discipline, led astray by his own great folly" (5:23). The wayward wife has "feet that go down to death," and her "steps lead straight to the grave. She gives no thought to the way of life; her paths are crooked, but she knows it not" (5:5-6).

What makes unfaithfulness such a big deal in God's eyes? Why the stern warnings? First of all, adultery breaks God's moral law. Unfaithfulness is not merely impractical; it is immoral. It's easy to lose sight of this. A divorced woman sought some help from me when I was a speaker at a camp. Back home in her church she was slowly becoming involved with a married man. The affair started with casual glances in the choir loft during practice. Seeing him privately and hearing of his affection for her was drawing her closer to a sexual encounter with him. She was startled, not because it was happening, but because it seemed so harmless. "When he tells me how attractive I am, I feel excited and good. When I'm with him, I'm so happy." How could something so good be so bad? That's what bothered her.

It's that mixture of good and bad that Proverbs portrays.

> For the lips of an adulteress drip honey, and her speech is smoother than oil; but in the end she is bitter as gall, sharp as a double-edged sword. (5:3-4)

We can muster all the practical reasons why infidelity is bad, but foremost, it is wrong because it's wrong. A panel of experts was once discussing extramarital sex. The sociologist and psychologist listened while the clergyman spoke first. "It's bad," he explained, "because of the mental anguish it can cause the partner; secondly, keeping sex within the home will make strong families, something society needs." Unexpectedly, he was cut off by the sociologist. "What in the h__ are you doing?" he shouted at the minister. The sociologist continued without giving the clergyman a chance to reply: "You are giving us practical reasons why infidelity is wrong. Leave that to us. You are a minister. You are supposed to say sex outside of marriage is wrong because God said: 'Thou shalt not commit adultery.' "

It seems old-fashioned to make unfaithfulness a moral issue these days. Contemporary society tends to validate its rules by scientific studies. But unfaithfulness is a breach of one of God's Ten Commandments and a sin against creation. When Jesus was asked about divorce, He found His answer in the time before the Law was given.

In the beginning, there was no divorce. When a man leaves his parents and cleaves to his wife, they become one flesh. "They are no longer two, but one," said Jesus. "What God has joined together, let man not separate" (Matt. 19:6).

Marriage is a contract. The wayward wife has forsaken the covenant of her God. It is a commitment to another person, but it is also a covenant linked to God. God is tied to the wedding pledge because it is He who created the "one flesh" relationship.

Because marriage is a divinely sanctioned tie, divorce was never part of God's plan. In the beginning, marriage was sealed by an irrevocable, unconditional contract. Jesus' teaching was so tough, His own disciples were stunned into saying: "It is better not to marry" (Matt. 19:10). They knew marriage could turn into a nightmare. Bad marriages are not only a modern phenomenon. Proverbs talks about terrible marriages: It is better to dwell in the wilderness than with a contentious and angry woman (21:19). The disciples were wondering if marriage was worth the risk if one couldn't get out of it.

Jesus assured them it was and that while the marriage bond is built into creation, it is not absolute. He gave one exception: when one's partner is adulterous. And the Apostle Paul gave another: when a Christian is deserted by an unbeliever. The believer is not in bondage, apparently meaning he or she is free to remarry (1 Cor. 7).

While these exceptions are debated, it is clear that it's acceptable for a person to separate from a harmful partner (even if one doesn't hold to divorce), and that when divorce does occur, it is not an unforgivable sin.

Prone to Wander
One thing is sure: God's ideal is that marriage be held together by an unconditional contract. It is given, not to burden us, but to bolster us in our efforts to make a marriage.

The Bible makes it clear that marriage needs some external forces to hold it intact. Temptation to be unfaithful is both inward and outward. The external is stressed in Proverbs. The other woman is a strong attraction: "With persuasive words she led him astray; she seduced him with her smooth talk" (7:21). "Like a bandit she lies in wait, and multiplies the unfaithful among men" (23:28). Modern society has within it many things to distract from and destroy marriages.

Not all of the forces are external, however. James tells us that "each one is tempted when, by his own evil desire, he is dragged away and enticed" (James 1:14). Proverbs warns about this desire: "Do not let your heart turn to her ways or stray into her paths" (7:25).

But Scripture is not simply asking us to follow a commandment blindly. God's warning doesn't just say *bad road*; it says *harmful destination.*

God will judge the unfaithful. "The upright will live in the land . . . but the wicked will be cut off from the land and the unfaithful will be torn from it" (2:21-22). It is even more clear in Proverbs 5:21-22: "For a man's ways are in full view of the Lord, and He examines all his paths. The evil deeds of a wicked man ensnare him; the cords of his sin hold him fast."

God's commandments are not whims of a powerful deity who wants to take the fun out of his creatures' lives. Proverbs gives a graphic picture of the ruinous consequences of adultery.

> Keep a path far from [the adulteress], do not go near the door of her house, lest you give your best strength to others and your years to one who is cruel, lest strangers

WHAT *COMMIT* MEANT 47

feast on your wealth and your toil enrich another man's house. At the end of your life you will groan, when your flesh and your body are spent. You will say, ". . . I have come to the brink of utter ruin in the midst of the whole assembly." (5:8-14)

Adultery promises poverty and physical harm. Much of the ruin is described in terms of death. The promiscuous woman's "feet go down to death; her steps lead straight to the grave" (5:5). The man who is involved with her is on a path that leads to death. She is a "deep pit . . . a narrow well" (23:27). Although she promises a feast with sweet water and delicious food, in reality the dead are in her house, and "her guests are in the depths of the grave" (9:17-18). The prostitute's path leads "to the spirits of the dead. None who go to her return or attain the paths of life" (2:18-19).

Death, in Proverbs, may have some reference to eternal death, but it applies to destruction in this life. Sex has the power to destroy lives and bring down the mighty: "Do not spend your strength on women, your vigor on those who ruin kings" (31:3). "Many are the victims she has brought down; her slain are a mighty throng, her house is a highway to the grave, leading down to the chambers of death" (7:26-27). Sexual intercourse with her is "bitter as gall, sharp as a double-edged sword" (5:4). In Hebrew, bitterness is equivalent to poison (Franz Delitzsch, *Biblical Commentary on the Proverbs of Solomon*, Wm. B. Eerdmans Publishing Co., vol. I, p. 120).

This is heavy stuff in an age when we can flick a switch and see actors on the daily soaps merrily playing their games of musical beds. TV viewers are made to feel cheated if they haven't. When the charming actor follows the shapely actress into her bedroom, there is no feeling for the tragic like that in the following verses of Proverbs:

All at once he followed her like an ox going to the slaughter, like a deer stepping into a noose till an arrow pierces his liver, like a bird darting into a snare, little knowing it will cost him his life. (7:22-23)

Our entertainment films seldom explore the dark side of promiscuity. The diseases that touch the body and the deep wounds of the soul are rarely exposed. Like the wayward wife of Proverbs, they seem too often to say, "Come . . . let's enjoy ourselves with love!" (7:18) Rarely do they tell us that "the adulteress preys upon your very life" (6:26).

Part of the ruin is the shame that unfaithfulness brings. Shame is somewhat different from guilt. Guilt is a feeling that we have when we break a moral law. Shame is something we feel when we look bad before others. Because we look bad, we feel bad. It is said of the man who commits adultery: "Blows and disgrace are his lot, and his shame will never be wiped away" (6:33).

The shame for the woman is depicted in Proverbs' description of the wayward wife. What woman wants to be like the girl in this picture? She forsakes her friend (2:17); breaks a covenant (2:17); does things that lead to the grave (5:5); leads others to death (7:27) and does so in the name of "love" (7:18); is secretive and deceptive, saying that her husband "has gone on a long journey" (7:19); is loud and defiant, never staying home (7:11); and is very brazen, entangling men with persuasive and seductive words (7:21).

Shame occurs for both the man and the woman. It erodes self-esteem. Perhaps one of the reasons so many feel so bad about themselves is shame. Sexual exploits scar a person's self-image. Even after a person has received God's forgiveness, it may take time for self-respect to return. A wife in her thirties told my wife of the battle she was having with shame. During her college years, she and her friends passed around a paperback book that urged them to do anything with any man. They swallowed its advice and followed its directions. She is now plagued with flashbacks that invade and mar her lovemaking with her husband. She is winning the battle, but it hasn't been easy.

Others suffer from a person's infidelity. There is no direct statement in Proverbs about the injury to the betrayed spouse. Allusions are made, however, as in the statement that the wayward wife has "left the partner of her youth" (2:17). Link that with the contrasting proverb about an excellent wife—"her husband has full confidence in her" (31:11). Proverbs 12:4 may be the most direct description of what the unfaithful woman does to her husband: "A disgraceful wife is like decay in his bones." Rottenness slowly spreading through the skeleton may symbolize the inner emotional pain a wounded spouse can feel. Seducing another person's spouse injures that person. The one who does so can't always make the excuse that he or she could not have done so if the marriage were not already dead. Elizabeth Taylor allegedly told Debbie Reynolds that she was not to blame for taking Reynolds' husband away from her. Had Eddie Fisher had a good marriage to Reynolds, she said, she could not have done it.

The Proverbs also remind the adulteress of the possible day of reckoning with the offended husband. "For jealousy arouses a husband's fury, and he will show no mercy when he takes revenge. He will not accept any compensation; he will refuse the bribe, however great it is" (6:34-35).

All this censuring of sexual affairs may give a lopsided view of marital faithfulness. Proverbs makes it clear that loyalty to your partner demands more than avoiding an affair with another; it requires having an affair with your spouse. Most of us will never commit adultery, but we will be unfaithful. Marriage is far more than living together; it is loving together. Research shows that marital distress precedes marital disruption. Neglect inside a marriage generates temptation outside. The satisfied rarely stray. This is one of the reasons why we should prize so highly the marital relationship. But we have yet to describe marriage. In the next chapter, we'll begin to sketch Proverbs' picture.

Chapter
FOUR

LOVE IN A NUPTIAL SHELL

> Ever be captivated by her love.
> PROVERBS 5:19

A nice four-letter word like *love* can cause a lot of anxiety. "I no longer love my wife; what should I do?" a young man asked me. Other questions followed quickly, punctuating the panic that showed on his face. Is it normal for love to just dissolve, vanish, evaporate—expire like a driver's license? And if and when it does, what does it mean? Had he married the wrong girl? Did he really love her in the first place? With feeling gone, could marriage survive; and if it did, would it be reduced to sharing a house with a friend, except for periodic romps in the bedroom relieving lust or conceiving kids?

If we placed notices of "lost love" in the newspapers, the lost and found section would bloat. There would be two kinds. Some would be like that of the man I just mentioned: "Love Lost: woke up this morning and realized I no longer love my wife." Another sort would be like what I've often heard from people seeking my help: "Lost: my husband's love. He told me today he no longer loves me. I don't know what to do, except to drag on feeling as if I've been crushed by a giant thumb."

It is generally thought that love between a man and a woman is unique. Most people get married because they have fallen in love. But they aren't certain they should continue to feel that same kind of love.

The Book of Proverbs speaks of love: "love covers over all wrongs," in contrast to hatred, which "stirs up dissension" (10:12). We are urged to love friends and wisdom, not pleasure and death. But marital love isn't mentioned often. It doesn't appear where we might expect it. Never is the "wife of noble character" said to love her husband. But marital love does shine brilliantly amidst the advice to husbands in the fifth chapter:

> May you rejoice in the wife of your youth. A loving doe, a graceful deer—may her breasts satisfy you always, may you ever be captivated by her love. (5:18-19)

It's obvious that love is to occupy center stage in marriage: a husband is to be captivated by his wife's love. But exactly what kind of love? Is this merely a reference to sexual pleasure?

Romantic Love in the Pages of the Ages

We will come back to the biblical answers after we have looked at the contemporary questions that swirl like gnats around the idea of love. The concept of romantic love is not new. Jacob, who lived thousands of years before Christ, loved a girl named Rachel so much that he served seven years to get her (her father's price), but "they seemed like only a few days to him because of his love for her" (Gen. 29:20). As the story goes, Jacob ended up with two wives. And Leah, the other wife, constantly battled for him to "love" her as much as he loved Rachel.

The oldest Greek literature refers to this type of love. Homer wrote of the love of Odysseus and Penelope. So deep was their love, so strong their desire to be together, that Odysseus pretends to be crazy when the army wants to recruit him and take him away. But they endure a long separation. The description of their reunion is one of the most moving romantic passages in literature.

> She flew weeping to his side, flung her arms about his neck and kissed him. . . . Then Odysseus in his turn melted, and wept as he clasped his dear and faithful wife to his bosom. As the sight of land is welcome to men who are swimming toward the shore, when Poseidon has wrecked their ship with fury of his winds and waves; a few alone reach the land, and thus, covered with brine, are thankful when they find themselves on firm ground and out of danger—even so was her husband welcome to her as she looked upon him and she could not tear her two fair arms from around his neck. (Homer, *The Odyssey*, translated by Samuel Butler, Pocket Books in Kenneth S. Pope, et al., *On Love and Loving*, Jossey-Bass Publishers, p. 9)

We still dream, sing, and talk of falling in love. Yet, modern people don't all seem to fall the same way. Two researchers asked forty-eight college students to write down some thoughts about love. After studying the data, they concluded in scientific jargon what we expected: "Romantic love is not a clear-cut singularly understood phenomenon" (Kazak, Anne E. and N. Dickon Reppucci, "Romantic Love as a Social Institution, in Pope, *On Love and Loving*, p. 213).

Love doesn't lend itself to simple analysis. The famous psychologist Sigmund Freud seemed rather puzzled by the whole matter. When asked to comment on it, he once said, "Up to the present I have not found the courage to make any broad statement on the essence of love and I think that our knowledge is not sufficient to do so" (Kenneth S. Pope, "Defining and Studying Romantic Love," in Pope, *On Love and Loving*, p. 3). Nor has everyone been ecstatic over it. Francis Bacon said dogmatically, "It isn't possible to love and be wise." A physician in the seventeenth century dubbed love a "disease" that subverts kingdoms; overthrows cities, towns, families; mars, corrupts, and makes a massacre of men.

He claimed that lightning, wars, fires, and plagues have not done as much mischief to mankind as what he called "this burning lust, this brutish passion" (Pope, *On Love and Loving*, p. 1).

Romantic Love: A Formula

Today's scientists are thankfully more positive about love. They have discovered some common threads in people's experiences of love. If we were to create a recipe for romantic love based on the current research, here's what we would have.

First, mix together two persons of the opposite sex. They need not know each other. Chemically, they will fuse together despite any previous experience with one another or similarities of background.

Not any man and woman will do, however. They should not be blood relatives (recall all that talk about kissing one's sister). Other than that it's tough to predict what two will fall for each other. Just keep throwing two people together until it happens. When it does you will usually know it; go to step two for indications.

Step two—observe the following: the two persons will suddenly become preoccupied with each other. That is, they will concentrate on each other with the undivided attention of a hound chasing a rabbit. They will want to spend a lot of time together, talking, laughing, and walking. There's no predicting what they'll do when with each other. Activity isn't what counts: what matters is intimacy. They may have a strong compulsion to jump into bed together, though their good sense may keep them from doing so. This sensual desire includes an emotional one that is somewhat like it. They'll want to strip off the layers of personality, like clothes, trying to see the inner nakedness. They'll delight in every new discovery, the more intimate, the better. But intimacy will be mixed with distance. The fact that they don't yet know a lot about each other adds an awesome mystery to the relationship. Without this "remoteness," the fusion is not so great. In fact, it is possible that as they learn more about each other, some of the excitement subsides.

They thrive on simple activities like "doing nothing" as long as they're doing it together. A good test at this time is to try separating them: if romantic love has occurred, they will be gloomy and depressed after a few hours or days and—let me warn you—very, very angry with you. You can tell if it is romantic love also because it usually happens quickly. It's this speed that will amaze you. When you get the right two parties, it "just happens." You'll hear them talk about "love at first sight." This is what makes it different from all of the other people you threw together who remained relative strangers. When love strikes, persons become intimate almost overnight. It's uncanny.

Another trait of this preoccupation with each other is that it is so enjoyable. There will be no complaining—no feeling of obligation. When the phone rings, they won't be saying to themselves, *Why does he have to call when I have all this homework to do?* They'll behave as if the other person is the only thing that matters. At this point, conflict with others is typical. A parent, boss, or friend will pressure the stricken one to "keep his nose to the grindstone." Self-control will become a problem. The lover will excuse dumb things or explain the neglect of duties with words like, "I couldn't help myself." If the lover shows little alarm at his or her lack of control, don't fret. This is normal.

The reaction will also be registered physically. Hook the proper instruments to your subjects and you will find that when they are near one another, the heart rate rises rapidly; x-rays will show butterflies in the stomach. You can observe other reactions: sweaty palms, weak knees, and even staggering caused by dizziness. All these symptoms are the same as those people have when under stress. Not to worry, however; all's normal.

There will be a certain "robustness" to the relationship. The relationship will not only rise quickly, it will be very

LOVE IN A NUPTIAL SHELL

tough. Romantic love is composed of some very strong human fibers. Once formed, it is not easily broken. You or others may try to pry your parties apart, but they'll stick. A consistency similar to taffy is typical at this stage. Remember Romeo and Juliet?

Keep in mind that the reaction won't last very long unless it involves both parties. True love includes both loving and being loved. If you perceive only one person "falling in love" when you put two together, separate the stricken one for a time while the "broken" heart mends. Blues music usually speeds the healing process, making the person ready to be placed with other persons with the hope that the next experience will be a duet rather than a solo. If not, follow the same procedure as the first time. Some persons, especially teenagers, go through a lot of this.

Somewhere during the reaction, you may be fooled into thinking that what is happening is quite selfish. But notice that a partner will display an awesome concern for the other's welfare. He will listen for long hours about her stressful conflicts at the office and yearn for her to get a happier job. She will pamper him and sometimes buy him presents or bail him out of problems at great financial cost. At times, they will appear as selfless as Mother Teresa. But self will still be in the picture. When the love bug bites, the lover will "enjoy" and "be thrilled" by unselfish acts lavishly poured out for the benefit of the loved. No sacrifice for the loved one creates a pain that is greater than the joy it brings. One expert claims, "One can speak of love only when consideration of the object goes so far that one's satisfaction is impossible without satisfying the object, too" (H.S. Sullivan, *Conceptions of Modern Psychiatry,* 2nd edition, Norton, pp. 42-43).

One more reaction will confirm that you have the right mix. Careful observation will show a strong tendency toward idealism. The lovers seem to have lost touch with reality. You may have noticed that at the first—when you put two people together you thought would never get along and suddenly they were calling each other "beautiful" and "wonderful." Two more unsightly, less wonderful people you never knew. Yet, they idealized each other. They will seem to be blind to each other's problems and faults, even though those flaws are quite obvious to all around them. The idealization extends to all of life. They live in a sort of fantasyland, full of optimism and happiness. When this occurs, the batch is done. You have a case of romantic love. Step back and look at it and notice too the slight movement under your feet. That's the world going around; romantic love has something to do with it, we are told.

Now, to our questions. Does the Bible confirm that romantic love is normal? And should married couples expect to have this kind of love in their marriages?

Romantic Love to Mature Love

We'll look first at the point of view that most people hold. Let's call it the "romantic love to mature love" viewpoint. Until recently, I held this view. In my book *Achieving the Impossible: Intimate Marriage* (Multnomah Press), I put it this way: "Romantic love will bring you to marriage, but marriage will bring you to mature love." People can't expect the degree of novelty, excitement, and ecstasy of early marriage to continue. The blush of first love is just too hot a level to maintain in the cold climate of marriage. Cool is mature. Love, like a developing insect, needs to metamorphose into something more stable and grown-up. Passionate love gives way to companionship love. Companionship love is more low-key than passionate love, being more like friendly affection and deep attachment.

Here's how one woman describes the journey from passion to companionship:

> When I fell in love I felt fantastic! I glowed, people said they never saw me look prettier or happier. . . . As it turned out I married Ted. We're still very happy and very

much in love, but there is a definite difference between the first passionate feelings of love and the now mellowed-out feelings.

Don't get me wrong, though, there are still plenty of passionate times. It's just that when you live together, the passion is not as urgent a thing. You're more loving friends. (Elaine and G. William Walster, *A New Look at Love,* Addison-Wesley, p. 4)

There is a troubling contradiction in this viewpoint. When two lovers scamper down the aisle after the wedding, they expect love to be forever. Yet, they're supposed to think it will somehow change. There's something puzzling about that. If love turns into companionship, is this the same love they believed would last? Is there really a different kind of love?

Romantic Love to Brotherly Love

The next view comes down much harder on romantic love. Call it the "romantic love gives way to brotherly love" viewpoint. It asserts that romantic love would be nice, but it's hardly essential. Chief advocate of this view, Mary Pride, states it this way: "Romance is the blossom on the flower of marriage, not the root. It is beautiful, it is a gift of God, but marriage can survive without it. Expecting romantic love makes kicks and thrills the reason for marriage" (*The Way Home,* Crossway Books, pp. 17-18).

The love we should strive for is "brotherly love," claims Mary Pride. "God requires young wives to 'love their husbands' (Titus 2:4), and the 'love' He asks from us is phileo love; brotherly love. It is based on our relationship, not our emotions" (p. 20).

I would have to agree with Mary Pride that a marriage can certainly survive without romance, and it's possible for two people to marry even though they have little romantic feeling beforehand. A wife's not feeling love toward her husband is no reason for leaving him. Nor does being unloved give grounds for divorce. The basis of marriage is commitment. But commitment to what? Is it merely a pledge to bear children and convey sisterly or brotherly love? Shouldn't we expect more, want more, and strive for more? Is the love of the wife the same as her love for her pastor? And while a husband might have to settle for that, should he not have hoped for more? Mary Pride seems to be describing the "minimal marriage"; our question deals with the ideal one.

Romantic Love to More Romantic Love
"The continuation and cultivation of romantic love" is what I call the third view. After years of marriage, a couple may not have the same *intensity* of love as at the beginning, but they can expect to have the same *kind* of love. If a couple had little romantic feeling to begin with, they can cultivate it.

Though I want to defend this view, I don't want to be dogmatic about it. Love is complex, existing in many forms and shades. Much like a summer sunset, just about anything anyone says about it is bound to be partly correct.

I see marital love as a special love we should strive for, according to the Scriptures. It has all the elements of the romantic love we talk about today, though there are some crucial differences. But in essence it's still romantic love, not some other kind of love that is supposed to replace it. It's more passionate than brotherly love and more thrilling than companionship love. Look closely at the advice to the husband in Proverbs 5:18-19:

> May you rejoice in the wife of your youth. A loving doe, a graceful deer—may her breasts satisfy you always, may you ever be captivated by her love.

The Hebrew word for love used here is used several times in Proverbs and many times in Song of Songs for the love between husband and wife. In this context, it stresses the

LOVE IN A NUPTIAL SHELL

sensuous side of love. But we should not conclude that the word refers only to erotic love in this passage or others. The love that captivates a man in marriage is broader than sex.

The word is used for the love Jacob had for Rachel, showing us how idealistic it can make a person feel. In love, Jacob was typically out of touch with reality when seven years went by seeming like a few days.

Love also includes intense preoccupation with another. That's the point Proverbs 5:19 makes: be preoccupied with your wife and don't give your attention to other women. And the attention is to be passionate. It is such that the husband is no longer in his own power; he can no longer restrain himself. "To be captivated" is the same word used for being intoxicated by wine (Franz Delitzsch, *Biblical Commentary on the Proverbs of Solomon,* Wm. B. Eerdmans Publishing Co., vol. I, p. 132). No labeling this "sisterly love." This is something special. In her husband's eyes the wife is to be a "loving doe" and a "graceful deer," both animals commonly used in ancient poetry as symbols of femininity because of the delicate beauty of their limbs and their sprightly black eyes. The prominent Old Testament scholar of the last century, Franz Delitzsch, writes of "an intensity of love connected with the feeling of superabundant happiness—'to be wholly captivated by her' " (*Biblical Commentary on the Proverbs,* vol. I, p. 131). The intensity of this love may sometimes make a person feel ill: "I am faint with love" (Song 2:5).

It might surprise us to find that this same word for love is used of God's love for His people (Deut. 7:8; 2 Chron. 2:11). "I have loved you with an everlasting love," says God through the Prophet Jeremiah (Jer. 31:3). "I led them . . . with ties of love," says God (Hosea 11:4).

Perhaps one of the reasons we dilute marital love of its passion is that we tend to see too many kinds of love. This is sometimes done by showing there are three biblical Greek words for love: *agape, phileo,* and *eros. Eros* is erotic love; *agape* is sacrificial love, and *phileo* is the love between friends. *Agape* is frequently distinguished from *phileo* especially in that *agape* is a willful love. Mary Pride distinguishes the kinds of love in this way, insisting that wives are to have a friendly or sisterly love for their husbands, since the command that they love their husbands uses the word *phileo* (Titus 2:4). Scholars now indicate that the words cannot be distinguished in this way. *Agape* is sometimes used of sensual love in Greek literature of New Testament times. We must be careful not to take the passion out of love, even God's love for us. God's love affair with Israel is nothing if it is not passionate.

Another ingredient of romantic love is present in the fifth chapter of Proverbs: enjoyment. No great sacrifice is required; the writer wants the man to enjoy. This is no command to reluctantly carry out a duty. His heart is to be in it. He is to rejoice in her. She is to be like a spring of water, flowing, refreshing, and invigorating. To express his joy, a husband might borrow a verse from the Song of Songs, "How delightful is your love. . . . How much more pleasing is your love than wine" (4:10).

Now we may be tempted to think that such words are only for the newly married man since the passage refers to his mate as the wife of his youth. But she is not the youthful wife; she is the present wife (now perhaps old) whom he married in his youth. He is never to forsake her. He is to keep the ecstasy in the marriage "ever" and "always."

Another component is there as well: both parties are involved. He is not to be passive but passionate. And she is not just a dutiful wife; she is like a "loving doe." Each loves and is loved. The word *love* reeks with the passion to merge. The origin of this mysterious yearning is found in chapter two of Genesis. After God makes a woman for Adam from one of his ribs, Moses says, "For this reason a man will leave his father and mother and shall be united to his wife, and they will become one flesh" (Gen. 2:24). The "reason" refers back to what God has just done. Adam and Eve had, in a sense, been one before—she being a rib. Their separation left them with a powerful desire to be one again. The desire to unite will be so powerful that a man will someday do the unthinkable: he will leave his father and mother. It's normal for a child to be so in love with his parents he will never want to separate from them. But the hormone flow at about age twelve performs wonders. His blooming desire to cleave to the opposite sex eventually anesthetizes any pain he has over leaving his parents. Marriage is to be an awesome experience of intimacy and merger—of becoming one, expressed in the words of Genesis 2:25: "The man and his wife were both naked, and they felt no shame." The sensual nakedness is symbolic of the more total nakedness. Couples are not merely to be joined in body, but also in soul. Biblical love, like romantic love, includes the strong desire to know the beloved as a person.

What of the robustness, the strength of romantic love—is that to be found in Scripture? The Song of Songs can be brought in as a witness to what Proverbs means since it was written during the same period of time:

> Love is as strong as death, its jealousy unyielding as the grave. It burns like blazing fire, like a mighty flame. Many waters cannot quench love; rivers cannot wash it away. (Song 8:6-7)

If love is like a blazing campfire, why do some couples have only a few cold embers left after four or five years of marriage? Love dies, unfortunately, not of suicide. People kill it.

Perhaps they do this by failing to add fuel to it, thinking love must happen by its own power and that there is little we can do to control it, since it is emotional in nature. As such, it's generally thought of as uncontrollable and unsustainable. You "get over it," and there is nothing you can do about it. And therefore, you shouldn't hold your partner accountable for feeling love toward you.

The greatest mistake we make about romantic love is thinking it is uncontrollable because it is emotional. We speak of it as "falling in love," as though it is like sprawling on the floor when a chair collapses under us. This can cause us to feel helpless in marriage. Persons don't take responsibility for what happens. If love somehow disappears in their marriage, they often disappear too. You fall in love, fall into bed, expectations fall short, you have a falling out, the marriage falls flat, you fall away, and one of you is the fall guy. And there was nothing that could be done about it. It is common for grown men and women to excuse themselves for an affair or for allowing their marriages to go cold by swearing they couldn't help themselves.

A recent film, *Falling in Love*, depicted two people with this frame of mind. On a subway, a man's eyes caught those of a woman, starting a love affair between these two married people. As the reels rolled, the couple tumbled into love. All the while the audience is led to cheer for them to leave their drab marriages and stumble helplessly and headlong into the new love. They are compelled to follow love, which summons them like a god. Previous commitments to morals or family are subjected to its power. Nothing else matters if one is struck by one of Cupid's priceless arrows. When it happens, obey it; it may never happen again.

People who think this way never really learn how to love; they only learn how to search for it. For them, love is something that happens, not something you make happen. Yet, the Bible urges us to make love. It's really not fair to your spouse to say in so many words, "I will act in love, but don't expect me to feel love." Isn't part of meeting our partner's need feeling love for them? If a husband dutifully takes his wife out for dinner because she needs his companionship, is that enough? Doesn't she have a need for him to need her companionship, to desire it?

Is the Bible saying that we have control over our affections as well as our actions? Are we not obliged to keep love alive? Even if we never really had a grand feeling of romantic love, we can still cultivate it as best we can.

So much of Scripture points in that direction. When God

asks us to love Him, it isn't just with our minds or wills. "Love the Lord your God with all your heart and with all your soul and with all your strength" (Deut. 6:5). In other words, part of loving is cultivating an affection for God. The same is true of other commands in Scripture. Repeatedly, the writer of Proverbs urges us to love wisdom: "Do not forsake wisdom, and she will protect you: love her, and she will watch over you" (Prov. 4:6). In this case love can't mean unselfishly doing something for someone; wisdom doesn't need anything from us. In fact it is for our sake that we are to love it: "Love her and she will watch over you." Obviously, the writer is telling us to have an affection for wisdom, delight in it, desire it, and value it as something precious. That's a *feeling* about wisdom we should cultivate.

The same applies to married love. When Paul tells husbands to "love their wives" (Eph. 5:25), he is not just telling them to act in love; he is telling them to cultivate their affections and keep love in their marriages. When wives are urged to be "husband-lovers," they are urged to generate warm affection for their husbands.

The hideous thing about the adulterous wife is that she has betrayed her partner. To abandon a lover is an unthinkable act. When God speaks through the Prophet Jeremiah of how Israel has betrayed Him like an adulterous woman, He says, "Have you not just called to me: 'My Father, my friend from my youth'" (Jer. 3:4). God is saying that one moment His people call to Him as a "friend," which is the same Hebrew word used in Proverbs 2:17, and the next moment they have forsaken Him.

It is somewhat a mystery how the passionate love of June can turn into hot anger by December. Yet, it happens all the time. My wife and I overheard an angry woman in an airport say what divorce attorneys hear most business days: "I want to take that sucker for all he's worth." How does a marriage turn a "lover" into a "sucker"? Sometimes love doesn't turn to anger, but simply to ashes. In the next chapter, we will explore ways of keeping that from happening.

Chapter
FIVE

FOREVER LOVERS

> Ever be captivated by her love.
> PROVERBS 5:19

"I have never seen my parents happier." This came from a daughter observing her middle-aged parents. "A few years ago they were almost divorced. Daddy was impossible. ...All I know is Mom just didn't give in to him, and now they're like kids together. Daddy brings her flowers; they've started playing golf together" (*McCall's*, July 1985, p. 148).

Second honeymoons do occur, even after decades of marriage. Couples rediscover their love for each other. But did they have to lose it in the first place?

Since Scripture tells us husbands and wives should have a special kind of love, they ought to do what they can to "make love." If a couple has a good dose of love before marriage, they need to hold on to it. Any fool can fall in love; it takes wisdom to stay in love. Even if love was nil before marriage, a couple should try to cultivate it, since sometimes love follows, instead of precedes, marriage. "Isaac... married Rebekah... and he loved her" (Gen. 24:67).

Lover Types
Perhaps a good way to begin improving yourself as a lover is to come to grips with your background. "I don't really know

what love is," a 21-year-old man said to me. We sat together on a beautiful southern California hillside at a conference grounds where he had heard me speak. He was tortured by this inability to fall in love. Though he had been dating girls since high school days, he never felt anything special for any of them. "What's it like to be in love?" he asked. "How will I know when it happens?"

I asked him about his family life. His next words, "I ran away from home when I was eighteen," didn't surprise me. The struggle with love is usually connected with past struggles in the family. "My dad never showed any affection for me," he continued. "A military man, he was a harsh disciplinarian." The young man explained how his mother didn't pour much love out to him either. He left home after an angry episode caused by his hairstyle. "My dad got so mad at my long hair, he began pulling it out by the roots while beating my head against the plaster." Hearing his screams, his mother stopped his father. The boy quickly fled the house, remembering the pain, confusion, and the hole in the kitchen wall his irate dad had used his head to make. "Do you think I'll ever feel love?" he asked. I offered him hope. "Certainly," I said. Our backgrounds tint our emotions as dye colors cloth, but the past's pigments are not indelible. They can fade, and our deepest self can undergo change. That is the message of the Gospel.

But the stain of that young man's past may always—to some degree—be with him. His experience of love may never be what it might have been. This is one of the reasons love is not the same for each of us.

Each of the following people has a different attitude toward love. Do you recognize yourself in any of them?

Joyce. After seven years, marriage was good for Joyce, but not secure. It wasn't for the lack of love for Phil. She was obsessed by him, clinging to him when together, dreaming of him when apart. Around other women, she felt jealous of him; when he was gone, she was anxious, wondering what he was up to. Her feelings fluctuated often, zooming to new heights when she was in his arms, plunging to the cellar whenever he was distant and indifferent toward her.

Phil complained of her smothering him and became frustrated over always having to prove he loved Joyce. To him she was an emotional extortioner, demanding affection and never getting enough.

Phil. Phil felt he did love Joyce. As a Christian he felt compelled to love his wife. He felt secure in his marriage to Joyce and couldn't for all his trying understand her daily doubting of his love. He hadn't a jealous bone in his body. Before marrying, he had been jilted. But it didn't depress him; he never went around moping, fearing he would lose in love. He had never permitted his moods to be determined by a woman's feelings about him. He couldn't understand why Joyce needed him to leave love notes around the house; he certainly didn't need them from her. He knew she loved him. Joyce never seemed to know this for sure. A compliment or a reassurance only lasted a few hours. He could pump her up with gooey words and acts of affection all day long; but when she went to sleep, it apparently all leaked out. The next day not only was she ready for more of the same, but she claimed she needed it. Phil was confused about Joyce's bottomless emotional pit and very tired of trying to fill it up with affection.

Pearl. She was a writer, a wife and . . . well, there wasn't time for much more. But *writer* is what she would underline if she were to compose her obituary. Being a wife was a high priority in her mind, but not so much in her heart. As a Christian author, she was aware of the need for loyalty to her husband, Russ. She sought to meet his needs. He didn't complain often, but he did tell her he thought she was holding something back, keeping herself from coming as close as he would have liked.

Pearl was in love with Russ, and she was committed to him, but not without reservation. Runaway love was something impractical, something to be avoided. She had taught herself to feel this way. She had built up her defenses against love as a turtle grows a shell. Love can hurt too much. She had seen too many broken-hearted girls in the college dorm. She would not be a slave to love. She had made promises to herself as a writer. What mattered most to her was that she would have control—or, more correctly, God would have control. She did not commit her love to Russ until she was certain he would not interfere with her goals. She wanted love, but with freedom. She wanted a relationship, but not with abandon. Love gave no right to one person to impose his or her will on another.

Pearl enjoyed her marriage for what it contributed to her. She was willing to give in return. Sex, for example, was something she offered to her husband. She enjoyed the closeness, but she really didn't enjoy sex that much. The thrill wasn't nearly as great as having a publisher accept one of her articles.

Jim and Kay. They were pretty much alike as far as love goes. They had married for love, and they weren't disappointed. Sex was like a fountain of warmth and closeness that spilled over into their whole relationship. It didn't matter what they were doing, they enjoyed being together. Their companionship was woven into the family times with the children. Through the years they grew more intimate. Though married for eight years, they still took delight in learning about each other. They thought of themselves as lovers and friends. No strong jealousy ever came between them, since trusting was easy for them.

Deal with the Past in Your Present
Out of the five people I've described, Jim and Kay are like most of us. Research shows that about fifty percent of married people have secure and fairly close relationships. Loving and being loved is no problem for them because they came from homes where they were loved. The other three most likely did not.

Joyce had problems in her childhood that made her into the "anxious lover." Love is an obsession for her. This makes her extremely possessive and often jealous. She simply can't trust. Her emotions are too tied to her husband's reactions to her. Her anxiety about love is rooted in her childhood. Anxious lovers report that one parent was coolly demanding and distant. Women had love from their mothers, but indifference and hostility from their fathers. For men it was the other way around. Dad was involved with them, but Mom wasn't.

Call Phil and Pearl "indifferent lovers." Pearl's indifference to love is more deliberate than Phil's. She has made herself into a "distant" partner. She holds to the modern notion that marriage must not interfere with her freedom. Whatever happens, she must remain in charge. She must not submit to love's control. Career is first. She knows that success in modern times goes to those who avoid heavy relationships. She can't afford to give in to her passions and emotions. When she was single, she learned to disengage from long relationships quickly, frequently, and without lingering pain. She would have to be in charge of her emotions if she was going to be successful.

Phil is also distant and indifferent, but for another reason. Instead of choosing to become emotionally detached, he was always that way. His inability to love deeply is due to his past relationship with his parents. As is true for anxious lovers, one or both parents rejected him. As a child he had to defend himself against the hurt he was constantly feeling. That defense took the form of a hard shell—an apathy toward intimacy. He convinced himself that he couldn't care less about love. Now, even when he knows he should love, he almost can't or won't. Deep love can cause deep hurt. His indifference is a shield of protection.

About one fourth of married persons are "anxious lovers" and another fourth "indifferent lovers." That means that half of us will have some serious problem with love.

Imagine what a marriage is like when a Phil marries a

Joyce. Joyce needs constant reminders that she is dearly loved; Phil is almost unable to love. Joyce wants to lose control to abandon herself to Phil. Phil is frightened about losing his autonomy and can't fully give himself to Joyce. He will have a hard time being "captivated by her love." But if he takes seriously God's command to love his wife, he can overcome his past. He must become aware that he has been shaped by his past and that he need not be locked into being this kind of person. His attitude and understanding are not normal, and he must learn to let go and deal with his fears of intimacy. Joyce, the anxious lover, will need to learn to control her mistrust and be gratified by the love she receives. Being aware of the origin of her anxiety may help her see that her husband isn't entirely the problem. She can take some pressure off him and work harder at seeing how he is showing his love.

Persons like Pearl will need to rethink their view of priorities as well as the nature of love. They will need to see the importance of the marriage commitment, recognizing that God calls us to love with abandon. "My lover is mine and I am his" (Song 2:16). Her choice not to let go of herself in her marriage prevents her body from letting go in bed, which is essential for enjoying sex.

We can now see why romantic love, as we see it in Scripture, is not everyone's experience. Our childhoods may have warped our ability to love. Growing up means learning how to love; some of us will struggle more with this than others.

Survive the Early Stages of Love

While staying in love is a special problem for some people, it will be a normal problem for all of us, simply because this is the nature of romantic love. Love, like a disease, goes through several stages, some very critical. Couples caught unaware of what is happening may react wrongly at a crucial point, damaging the growing relationship.

We are fairly certain of the stages. The first is that exciting "falling in love" phase. In chapter three we described the things that happen: the passion to know, to be united, and to be with each other; and the joyful preoccupation with each other's life and welfare. And there is one quirk that is the greatest catalyst for love's changes: idealism. Love is like a drug that attacks the brain, distorting the lover's view of reality. One researcher maintains that this is caused by the feeling that our partner "completes us." Before our plunge into love, we see ourselves as imperfect and incomplete. Our lover now raises us to the level of being "self-sufficient, all-powerful and omniscient—in a word, perfect" (Steven Friedlander and Delmont C. Morrison, "Childhood," in Kenneth S. Pope, et al., *On Love and Loving*, Jossey-Bass Publishers, p. 29). Our euphoria over our newfound completeness makes us partially blind to our partner's faults. That we don't fully know our lover is of little concern. We are like the man so taken by the color of the used car that he takes for granted that the rest of it will be OK.

This idealization leads to a second stage in marriage, as it does with the buyer of the used car. Call it "disillusionment." The tunnel of love can lead to the cellar of disappointment when reality sets in. Not only do the person's flaws come in focus, but they may even make us doubt our love. Coming to know someone in the intimacies of marital life can be rudely shocking. The physical things we have come to accept in ourselves are not as easily accepted in someone else: "the burps, snorts, wrinkles, sweat, moles, urination and defecation—these can turn us off or give us pause" (Kenneth S. Pope, "Defining and Studying Romantic Love," in Pope, *On Love and Loving*, p. 7).

Awakened on his honeymoon night, a husband discovered his bride snoring. "I didn't even know women snored," he said. Poetically he could have said:

Oh, how my disappointment soars:
Silvia, Silvia, Silvia snores.

Generally, though, the full impact of the second stage comes somewhere during the second year of marriage. If some disappointments were all there were in the second stage, it wouldn't be so bad. But lovers can become aliens. They can become angry about what they have discovered the other to be. The differences produce conflict, the conflict creates anger, the anger breeds arguments and bad feelings. All the while they are blaming each other rather than the idealized pictures in their minds. "If only you weren't like this." "I was like this when you married me." "You were not." Most couples make it through this stage; some don't. If they stay together, they will arrive at stage three.

Call this the "realistic stage." Ideal views of one another give way to realistic ones. They now love each other for what they are and not for what they thought each other to be. This is a "mature love." As I mentioned earlier, some researchers think this is a different kind of love, but I don't think the Bible makes such a distinction.

Some arrive at stage three with very little left of the original love. The fire and smoke of stage two have scorched their feelings beyond recognition. Stage one dreams have turned into stage two nightmares. Romantic love *can* survive stage two. There is evidence that in most marriages stage three love is not entirely different from stage one love. Much of the idealistic picture they had is gone, but the rose-colored glasses remain, put there by the couple's passion for one another. Those who triumph at stage three follow some guidelines like the following.

Guideline one: Stress the positive side. Some marriages go bad simply because they focus on the bad. One researcher has discovered three steps to the divorce court: first, the quarreling becomes destructive to both persons; second, affection is withheld and loving responses decline; and third, divorce as an option is mentioned and considered (Daniel Goleman, "Heart of Cupid: Love Ills, Thrills Tied to Childhood," *The Arizona Republic,* Sunday, Sept. 22, 1985, section AA, p. 11).

I sat at a kitchen table with a couple that had definitely passed the first two steps. After six years of marriage the conflict between them was hurtful and damaging. Anyone who knew them well before marriage could have predicted they were destined for a head-on collision. She was aggressive and often unyielding, a strong leader. He was a follower: he didn't relish taking the initiative. He wanted to take things more slowly. "Paint the house? Oh, let's wait; we'll get around to it," he would say. Her reaction would be, "Oh, no, it's got to be done—now." She was driven; he wasn't. He was laid back; she was leaping forward. She opposed his suggestion to go out for dinner. "No," she said violently. "It costs too much." When he kept on insisting, she finally demurred. But by then he wasn't in the mood to eat—anywhere. He resented her resisting his ideas and pushing hers. Bitter feelings were filling their home like smoke, making it hard for them to see much good in their marriage. Marriage was a hassle; everything was a hassle.

Wisely, they were working on the conflict. They had seen a counselor and were trying hard to follow his advice. Did I have any suggestions? they asked me. Only one. Work on the good side of your marriage. Revelation 3:2 advises, "Strengthen what remains and is about to die." It's spoken to a congregation, not a couple. Christ commanded them to look at what was good and make it stronger. The principle can apply to marriage too. Whatever is left, make it better.

There are two ingredients in every marriage: the attracting and the repelling. Couples must learn to deal with those things that tend to drive them apart. But in the process they shouldn't neglect those things that make their relationship something great. If the bad destroys the good, what is left? "Granted, a lot of conflict has hurt you and your relationship," I told them. "But what remains?" They both agreed that they had some good companionship, especially with the children. "And what about your sexual, love life?" I asked. "Oh, whenever we do it, it's great. We often say to each other afterward, 'We ought to do this more often.'" They thought of more fun, good things they loved about each other. They were like two kids who were finding their way back on a merry-go-round, wondering why they had gotten off.

At the disappointing stage two, many couples just let things fall apart. Trouble, like an intruding stranger, pushes his way between them. Instead of passionately clinging to one another, they weaken their grip. Numerous women, for example, have asked me if it was right for them to have sex with husbands who showed absolutely no affection for them outside the bedroom. "The only thing he wants from me is my body," is the way they put it. Resentment makes them want to get back by holding out. "Strengthen what remains," I tell them. Their husbands are like ships being pulled from their moorings by hurricane winds. All the ropes that held them are broken but one, which is unraveling. Cut that cord and the storm takes the ships. To fight the tempests and squalls of marriage, we must toughen the fibers that connect us.

Guideline two: Work at it. There is a tendency to think love is spontaneous and effortless. If we have to plan, struggle, toil, bear down, and work at it, forget it. That takes the kick out of it. Other things are work, but not love. Tell the new mayor he has a tough road ahead, and he'll accept it. Say to a new surgeon, "You are entering a demanding profession," and he'll agree. But tell a new husband, "You have a tough job ahead of you," and he'll probably think you're joking or criticizing his new bride. But marriage demands a commitment to work as much as any profession or job.

Guideline three: Be flexible. To stay in love, you need to be willing and eager to change. Keeping love alive doesn't merely require holding on to past feelings; it demands generating new ones. You can't stay in a rut and stay in love—even if the original rut was terrific.

Love, like bread, has to be made daily if it's going to be fresh. One wife told me her mother ridiculed her for attending a marriage seminar. "After twelve years of marriage, you ought to know everything about it." Her mother was like a mountain climber who stopped at the first or second level rather than reach for the summit.

In other areas of life, we know that to move ahead we must press ahead. When learning to swim or play the piano, we expect to go from one level to the next. Growth is uneven; when we arrive at one stage, it seems to take a new, major spurt to get to the next. Then it's tempting to give up and be satisfied with where we are. There must be an awful lot of people like me who never got beyond the second grade book of *John Thompson's Modern Course for the Piano*.

When it comes to playing a musical instrument, stopping is not necessarily all that bad. Not all the hands that learn to plunk "Row, Row, Row Your Boat" are destined to play Beethoven's *Fifth Piano Concerto*. But do we have that kind of option in marriage? What have we got to say for our marriage if after fifteen years we are still at an elementary level? "This is Jane. This is Joe. Jane is Joe's wife. Joe is Jane's husband. See Jane wash dishes. See Joe read the newspaper. Wash, Jane, wash. Read, Joe, read."

Keeping the boredom out of marriage means keeping the newness in. Being a growing person keeps you from being stale and your marriage from being dull. Part of what love is all about is the enjoyment and excitement of being involved with a new and exciting person. In other words, we enjoy and respond to the newness we find in each other and in our relationship. Granted, it's not all fun; love includes sacrifice, sweat, and tears. Often, in our attempt to help our partner reach goals and satisfy needs, it will cost us plenty. To be good lovers we must lose ourselves. It's love that takes the sting out of sacrifice. We will "enjoy" being absorbed in our companion's welfare. "It is more blessed to give than to receive" (Acts 20:35).

As renewed persons in renewed marriages we maintain renewed love. To be fresh we must be flexible. There are many ways we can keep on being renewed and interesting persons. Personal growth in any area can inject new life into our marriage relationships. A friend just told us about the dramatic change in his middle-aged mother. After a lifetime of fear about travel she made an international trip, motivated mostly by the desire to see her daughter, a missionary in the Philippines. Friends and relatives were surprised to see her step on a plane, fighting the feeling of insecurity that had kept her virtually imprisoned in her hometown. The trip's results were equally surprising. She returned with a new sense of self, a more confident, resourceful, independent woman, who had made new discoveries about her herself and her world.

A husband and wife can deliberately try to make themselves more interesting to each other by experiencing things separately so that they have something to talk about when they are together. They can share what they've experienced from books, adult education classes, sporting events, and so on.

Guideline four: Recognize that what we value most in love may change through the years. Love, like an automobile, has many features. Certain aspects matter at one point in life that don't matter as much later. When young, a person may value the car's speed or classic lines. Later—a roomy interior and riding comfort. One researcher says love is like that. Passion peaks in the early phases of the relationship, but declines to a plateau. Intimacy becomes more crucial as time goes by. Then, in a third phase, understanding and support become the crucial items. Intimacy increases, and throughout all stages passion remains, but the emphases on the different facets of love tend to change. If the persons in love don't flex with the different needs, dissatisfaction sets in. Robert Sternberg claims that this failure to grow is a major cause of marital break-up. The divorce rate is so high, he writes, "not because people make foolish choices but because they are drawn together for reasons that matter less as time goes on" (quoted by Daniel Goleman, "Heart of Cupid," p. 1).

For example, a man's likes and dislikes in marriage change

through the years. A thirty-year-old man wanted a wife with the ability to share her thoughts and to be someone he could be genuinely interested in. A man of this age needs a companion who will stimulate him. However, fifty-year-old men spoke of their need for women who were kind, sociable, relaxed, poised, and warm. They were looking for caring companions.

If the importance of the ingredients changes, the individuals in the relationships must try to change. Suppose in the early years of marriage a woman is thrilled that her husband is so good at making love. Now she wants him to be good at making conversation. That puts the partner in a bind, since passionate sex may be a lot easier for him than intelligent talk. Changing may be very demanding. We don't all have the capacity to be whatever our mates want, but the dynamic character of married life requires that we try to change as best we can to keep love blazing. One marital expert puts it plainly: "You have to work constantly at rejuvenating a relationship" (Robert Sternberg, quoted in Goleman, "Heart of Cupid," p. 1).

Chapter
SIX

LOVE: THE RIGHT STUFF

> Better... vegetables where there is love.
> PROVERBS 15:17

Love is so important, we'd give up prime rib for it. Given the choice, Proverbs 15:17 says we would: "Better is a meal of vegetables where there is love than a fattened calf with hatred." Special affection between married partners is what the word *love* refers to in that verse. In another proverb its importance is stressed by its absence. An unloved spouse is enough to cause an earthquake.

> Under three things the earth trembles, under four it cannot bear up: a servant who becomes king, a fool who is full of food, an unloved woman who is married, and a maidservant who displaces her mistress (30:21-23).

Love: Inside and Out

Marital love can be divided into the external and internal aspects. Internal matters are the emotional ways we show love: making love, sharing intimate thoughts, expressing feelings, saying we care. Externals are bound up in the marital duties and tasks: making a living, cooking meals, having babies, fixing the plumbing.

In the past perhaps externals mattered most. Caught in

changing times, the dairyman, Tevye, in the beloved musical, *Fiddler on the Roof,* asks his wife, "Do you love me?" "I'm your wife," she replies. "I know—but do you love me?" he asks again. "Do I love him?" she mutters. "For twenty-five years I've lived with him, fought with him, starved with him. Twenty-five years my bed is his. If that's not love, what is?"

Today, the shift is to internal benefits. We focus more on a man's bringing home flowers than "bringing home the bacon." A wife wants a man who will do more than work; she wants him to talk. A husband wants romance, not just a roast for supper. This switch has created a revolution of sorts. Marriage is more demanding, since a man may be more prepared to be a provider than he is to be an intimate friend. Marriage is also more confusing and controversial since we aren't sure what to expect.

Biblically, it's obvious that we are to expect both. A man is expected to be a caring partner, not just a careful provider. A wife is to be cuddly, not just competent; amorous, not just able.

The best way to turn marriage into a humdrum mechanical thing is to stress the duties and roles. Even sex becomes one more job, like vacuuming the carpet. Books and movies give this picture of marriage. Often, romance and sex are placed before and outside of marriage. Marriage is dull and practical. When I shared this once in a seminar, a woman shared a profound insight with the group. In marriage, she explained, we should not only aim at having both the external and internal expressions of love, but we should think of throwing them together. The secret in marriage is to mix intimacy and duty, lovemaking and homemaking. She described a recent film to make her point that the world doesn't often see it that way. *Same Time Next Year* told of two married people who have an adulterous affair with one another. Each year a summer cottage became the scene of their two-week-long annual liaison. Then they returned to their unromantic family life, waiting for next year's two-week affair. Romance and intimacy came easily with someone with whom they didn't share the responsibilities and hassles of married life.

The Bible declares a man's mistress should be his wife; that a woman's husband should be her lover. It's not easy to squeeze some romantic moments into the daily routine of cooking, scrubbing, cleaning, and keeping drawers and closets neat. Balancing a budget, scolding kids, wiping noses, cleaning a cellar, and washing a skinned knee can crowd out long, intimate talks. But that's the challenge of marriage. A real lover can one day clean a sick spouse's vomit off the floor and another relish his or her kisses. The good husband sees no contradiction in nursing a sick wife and making love to her. A good wife can be a "mom" during the day and a "sweetheart" at night. Good marriages are made by people who learn to be faithful to both the external and the internal demands. Not that it won't be difficult, particularly when the externals take so much energy and time.

To keep both the inner and outer expressions of love in a marriage, a couple will need to value both. Too often, a person puts one above the other or pits one against the other. I tried in vain to make a husband see that he needed to show his wife more affection. He wasn't willing to say, "I love you." She was starved for expressions of intimacy. All the while she yearned for these signs of affection, he kept trying to convince her he was showing his love by remodeling the house and making a good living. He was not willing to cultivate other ways to show love. On the other hand, some partners are quite affectionate, but not very dependable. I know men who say, "I love you," but who need to say more often, "I'll help you."

In this chapter, we are going to look at the external expressions of love in marriage. In the following chapters, the internal will be dealt with, particularly sex and intimacy.

Smart Love

Proverbs urges us to show our love. Having it isn't enough. "Better is open rebuke than hidden love" (27:5). In this case, love is expressed in constructive criticism. The proverb is telling us not to be afraid to rebuke. Not criticizing is not loving. Granted, it's more likely we will withhold love when it comes to criticism than we would otherwise. But in marriage we often don't do the loving thing; we don't communicate our love and it remains "hidden." It is clearly possible to have love and not show it because of being too fearful, too busy, or too insensitive. Often couples don't communicate their affection because they love in their terms rather than their spouses'. It's as if they are each speaking a different language. He thinks saying "I love you" is said by spending money for candy; she thinks it's said by spending time with her. He goes on saying it his way and she keeps on saying she doesn't feel loved. Our task is to learn each other's language of love. A friend of mine learned that offering to help his wife turns her on more than anything. He's a wise man, one who has studied his wife to discover her idea of love. One of the ways to find out how your spouse wants to be loved is to watch how he or she loves. If your wife shows love by baking a pie for you when you're feeling down, she will probably be thrilled when you do something to cheer her up when she needs it.

Another way to discover how your spouse wants to be loved is to watch for his or her responses, being careful to be as objective as possible. We need to give our spouses freedom to react honestly and not blame them if they don't see our expression of love as we do. A friend told a group of us about his doing what he aptly called "dumb love." He had poured years of energy into showing his love for his ill wife by routinely cleaning the house on Saturdays. When finished, he carried her from the bedroom to show her the shiny woodwork and clean floors. After more than twenty years of marriage, she finally told him what this meant to her. It meant humiliation. The tour of her freshly cleaned home only increased her sense of shame at not being able to do it herself. What he thought was a show of love was cause for embarrassment. How it hurt that she never told him—and that he never learned. Another way to learn our partner's language of love is simply to ask. It can be made easier by doing it in writing. Ask your partner to write five or ten of the most important things you do that make him or her feel loved. Then compare it to what you are doing—and be ready for a surprise.

Functional Love
A vital part of love is being responsible. In marriage each is dependent upon the other and therefore faithfulness to duties is crucial. If proverbs were pictures, snapshots of the ideal wife would show her doing a lot for her husband. Note how energetic and resourceful she is.

> A wife of noble character who can find? She is worth far more than rubies. Her husband has full confidence in her and lacks nothing of value. She brings him good, not harm, all the days of her life. She selects wool and flax and works with eager hands. She is like the merchant ships, bringing her food from afar. She gets up while it is still dark; she provides food for her family and portions for her servant girls. (31:10-15)

One of her enterprises is a vineyard: "She considers a field and buys it; out of her earnings she plants a vineyard" (31:16). "The woman apparently does buy and sell land," writes one Old Testament scholar. But, making the verse mean this falls into the hands of modern feminists, claims one author. "Tell me how buying shoes for your family makes you a shoe salesman, and I'll be able to explain to you how buying a vineyard makes this woman a real-estate dealer!" she objects. "Christian magazine articles and books commonly refer to her as such, but this makes no sense. She bought one field for her family's use; she didn't resell it, much less make a career out of buying fields here and there" (Mary Pride, *The Way Home,* Crossway Books, p. 149). I agree with this author that buying one field doesn't make this wife a real-estate agent. But I disagree with her insistence that everything a wife does must be done in the home and for her family. This noble wife in Proverbs obviously has to leave the house to buy land, plant a vineyard, and select wool and flax. And she does more than serve her family, extending her arms to the poor and her hands to the needy (v. 20). Before modern times, wives were involved in the economics of a family. Today's issue is not whether a wife works outside the home, but whether or not she neglects her family to do so. But the same is also true for the man. Feminists tend to demean the role of homemaker to elevate the career woman. Reacting to this, we should be careful not to degrade the working woman when we praise the faithful wife. Proverbs is saying what we should be shouting: Up with the homemakers! This noble homemaker "sets about her work vigorously; her arms are strong for her tasks" (31:17). She manufactures items to sell to businessmen: "She makes linen garments and sells them, and supplies the merchants with sashes" (31:24). She teaches her children and others: "She speaks with wisdom, and faithful instruction is on her tongue" (31:26). Lazy she is not: "She watches over the affairs of her household and does not eat the bread of idleness" (31:27).

If there were a wives' hall of fame, a statue of this hard-working, talented woman would grace the lobby. Notice that all of her activity adds up to one great reward for her husband: "Her husband has full confidence in her" (v. 11). In other words, he can depend on her. That kind of trust makes for a stable marriage and peace of mind. In contrast, one proverb portrays how painful it is to live with an unreliable person: "Like a bad tooth or a lame foot is reliance on the unfaithful in times of trouble" (25:19).

Love in Miniature
Perhaps the reason husbands and wives get disturbed about neglected duties is that it symbolizes something larger—the

lack of help when it's badly needed. A wife's failure to make a phone call in good times could make a husband question her dependability during tough times. It's well known that crises cause more marital discord and break-up than anything. Bad times magnify our personal weaknesses. If a person can't depend on us then, it's like having to chew on an aching molar or stumbling along on a lame leg.

Not being faithful to the little chores might indicate something else: lack of love. Not that love is absent; it's just not displayed. My taking out the garbage is a case in point. Now that all three of our boys have gone, I am superintendent of rubbish. But it's hard for me to remember that the containers are to be out on the curb Sunday and Wednesday nights. It's hard, not because I have more important things to do or because I have a bad memory. It's hard for me because I don't rank it high enough on my priority list. Not getting the cans to the curb doesn't affect me as much as it does my wife. If the cans fill up because I fail, Ginger has to put up with the inconvenience that causes. Instead of dumping the waste baskets into the containers and slamming the lid, she has to stomp it down and put some in plastic bags, which is troublesome, especially when the garage temperature is hovering around zero. When the garbage detail belonged to one of our boys, I rose to my wife's defense when they missed setting out the cans, scolding them for not living up to their God-given, family-bestowed responsibility, muttering at times, "You can't depend on these teenagers for anything." Now my neglect might occasion my wife's muttering to herself, though Ginger is very patient with me. Now, I'm the culprit. To be reliable, I must remind myself how important it is that I display my love to Ginger by doing the little things that are a big deal to her. Proverbs 20:6 touches on this very thing. "Many a man claims to have unfailing love, but a faithful man who can find?"

If a man says, "I'll love you forever, " but puts off fixing the dishwasher forever, what is his wife to think? Or if a woman whispers sweet things but serves tasteless meals, what's she really saying to her husband? John says, "Let us not love with words or tongue but with actions and in truth" (1 John 3:18). I tried to get this across to a young husband whose wife accused him of being "more willing to run out and fix someone else's sink than mine." He was quick to abandon a promised few hours with her if a phone call brought a plea for help. In turn, he blamed her for not caring about others. Many a doctor's wife and clergyman's wife have been so accused. What he failed to see is how his lack of dependability was interfering with his signals of love. A loving husband doesn't put the concerns of others above those of his wife. He calls if he is going to be late for dinner. He mails a letter on time if he says he will. It works the other way around too. In the afternoon a loving wife takes a nap (when possible) so she'll be up to making love in the evening. These little things contain a big message. We must not confuse small with insignificant, forgetting that love comes in small packages.

Sometimes our unreliability is a result of taking our spouses for granted. We think a good wife is supposed to understand why her husband canceled their evening out; a loving husband is supposed to be sympathetic about being crowded out of his wife's busy schedule. We neglect our duties, and our spouses feel neglected. Our failures wound them, and we blame them for bleeding. Not that we shouldn't forgive when we're the wounded ones. "Love covers over all wrongs" (Prov. 10:12). But counting on our partners' forgiveness as an excuse for failing them is like a presumptuous sin, when a person flagrantly sins because God has promised to forgive. It's one thing to say, "I goofed, but please forgive me"; it's another to think, "You'll forgive me, so I'll goof."

It may appear as if the proverbs are picking on the wives, since there is no portrait of the husband of noble character to match that of the "noble wife." In no way does this suggest the Old Testament is unfairly pressuring women to measure up more than it is men. Scores of proverbs speak to men, most of them applicable to husbands, and the standards they hold out are very high.

The proverbs judge the lazy man just as they praise the industrious woman. "The lazy man does not roast his game, but the diligent man prizes his possessions" (12:27). "One who is slack in his work is brother to the one who destroys" (18:9). I wonder if the writer didn't have a slothful husband in mind when he wrote, "The sluggard says, 'There is a lion outside!' or, 'I will be murdered in the streets' " (22:13). The fear of wild beasts in the streets didn't really keep ancient people home. This is probably a lazy man's excuse for not going out to find a job.

The cure for the lazy lies in a trip to an anthill.

> Go to the ant, you sluggard; consider its ways and be wise! It has no commander, no overseer or ruler, yet it stores its provisions in summer and gathers its food at harvest. How long will you lie there, you sluggard? When will you get up from your sleep? A little sleep, a little slumber, a little folding of the hands to rest—and poverty will come on you like a bandit and scarcity like an armed man. (6:6-11)

Like the good wife, the husband prepares for the future, as the ant stores its food for winter. He doesn't just talk, he acts. "All hard work brings a profit, but mere talk leads only to poverty" (14:23).

Seeing labor as love can help take the drudgery out of it. Whatever we do, it is to be done heartily unto the Lord (Col. 3:23). When others are involved, it is to be done in love. This puts a halo around things like fixing meals, unclogging sinks, cleaning basements, and washing cars. This can put meaning into menial jobs and difficult vocations. All work has dignity when it is done for others. I am sure that this thought alone keeps some men and women at tedious, boring jobs in modern factories, and it is surely an encouragement to mothers of diaper-clad children.

Skillful Love

Love demands more than loyalty to duties. Proverbs highlights the interpersonal skills love requires. The person who can't relate to others properly can make life miserable. "Better to live on a corner of the roof than share a house with a quarrelsome wife" (21:9; 25:24). The roof's corner might be just a figure of speech, picturing the discomfort (especially in stormy weather) that is preferred to life with an ill-tempered woman. It more likely is a literal description of the flat roofs people slept on in hot weather. That this identical proverb occurs in two places may give it emphasis. In case that isn't enough, the same idea appears in a third place, in Proverbs 21:19: "Better to live in a desert than with a quarrelsome and ill-tempered wife." Your own little spot in a desert or on a roof, lonely as it may be, beats living with a mean woman.

Living with a mean man is no picnic, either. A man can keep the hostile home fires burning. "As charcoal to embers and as wood to fire, so is a quarrelsome man for kindling strife" (26:21). We'll come back to this in a later chapter about conflict.

Conveying patience. Patience is one of love's offspring that can combat the contentious attitude. "Better a patient man than a warrior, a man who controls his temper than one who takes a city" (16:32). That controlling anger is better than becoming a war hero or making great military conquests shows how highly rated patience is in God's eyes. The person that controls his temper "has great understanding, but a quick-tempered man displays folly" (14:29). "A man's wisdom gives him patience" (19:11). Being patient will add luster to your image: "It is to his glory to overlook an offense" (19:11).

Anger may be the acid that most eats away at marital ties. Ask most people what destroys marriages, and chances are they would say, lack of communication. But the Bible challenges that idea, as does current research. There is something more basic than communication. One researcher calls it "positive regard." In a small study of both rural and urban couples, Howard Barnes concluded that regard was the most important factor in explaining marital satisfaction ("Positive Regard in Marriage," *Bulletin of the Washington County Extension Service,* Minnesota). "Regard is respect, positive feelings, admiration for the other person. . . . It is the basic emotional stance from which you are operating in your relationships," says Barnes. It is also the basic emotional stance with which 90%, if not all, couples begin their marriages. For some, the discord and differences pump seething, caustic anger into their veins. Slowly it makes its way to the heart to corrode the positive feeling, turning it negative. Love sours. Without positive regard, communication does little good, since most messages are tainted by ill feeling. Patience is the antidote to this poison. Patience means being slow to anger. It requires being kind when your spouse doesn't deserve it.

Being sensitive. A patient love will also be a sensitive one. One proverb tells of the importance of being in touch with another person's feelings:

> Like one who takes away a garment on a cold day, or like vinegar poured on soda, is one who sings songs to a heavy heart (25:20).

It's as cruel to respond wrongly to a grieving person as it is to tear someone's jacket off them on a winter day. Pouring vinegar on soda illustrates how destructive insensitivity is, since doing so destroys both the vinegar and the soda (Franz Delitzsch, *Biblical Commentary on the Proverbs of Solomon,* Wm. B. Eerdmans Publishing Co., vol. II, p. 166).

Nothing hurts worse than being misunderstood. When counseling couples, the words I hear the most are, "He (or she) just doesn't understand me." By these words they mean that their spouses don't react properly to their feelings. "I tell her I'm feeling down, and she quotes a Bible verse to me." "I explain to him that I'm not in the mood for making love, and he goes to pieces."

In marriage we need to talk about our feelings so that our partners can do or say the right thing. We should be asking each other questions like, When you are depressed, how do you feel? What don't you want people to do or say? What do you want from others?

In my seminars I've asked women to explain what they would like their husbands to do in the following situation: Your husband comes home to find you in a state of mild depression. You are supposed to go visit friends. Should he insist on your keeping the engagement? Some women say, "No, when I'm depressed, I need to be alone; the last thing I need is to go out." Just as dogmatically other women will say, "I need my husband to insist we go out with our friends; when I'm in the emotional cellar, I need someone to grab me by the arm and say, let's go." That some women want exactly the opposite of others shows that to be sensitive to a person you have to study that person.

Giving praise. Love will also express itself in praise. The wife of noble character has a husband who "praises her" (31:28). Husbands and wives should commend each other in private and laud one another in public. Charlie Shedd cunningly advises the new husband to lavishly praise his wife to his mother-in-law. When the wife later hears it from her mother, she'll feel great. Shedd's point is a good one. Discover the right moments and the right ways to honor one another—mail a thank-you note or leave one under the pillow; offer thanks for your mate at a prayer meeting or when you pray together; compliment him or her when with friends; acknowledge your mate's support when given credit for something you've done.

When we look for opportunities to praise, we will discover more about our spouses that is praiseworthy. Finding something that is laudable may take some concentration, not because of our partner's faults, but because of our blindness. Marriage seems to increase our ability to find faults more than to recognize strengths. This has been true of me. Being positive demands special effort. Periodically, I list Ginger's good qualities. I'll observe her as if I were watching a stranger, sharpening my ability to see new things about her. My appreciation soars, and I share it with her in the days that follow.

Being positive about your spouse excludes public criticism. Love demands that we protect each other's reputation. "Love covers over all wrongs" means keeping quiet about a person's failures (10:12). Women who complain about their husbands to others are as foolish as husbands who never commend their wives in public.

Projecting cheer. To end this chapter on a happy note, let's look at one more valuable interpersonal skill: being cheerful. "A cheerful heart is good medicine, but a crushed spirit dries up the bones" (Prov. 17:22). In a remarkable way, Norman Cousins recently proved the truth of this proverb. Seriously ill, he reasoned that positive feelings would lead to positive changes in his body. This insight led him to his now famous laughing therapy. Watching "Candid Camera" programs and Marx Brothers films reduced his pain and had a positive effect on his body chemistry (Norman Cousins, *Anatomy of an Illness,* Norton, 1979, pp. 35-40). The heart is where happiness begins, indicating that it's our attitude and not just our circumstances that creates cheerfulness.

"A happy heart makes the face cheerful, but heartache crushes the spirit" (15:13). If you're cheery on the outside, you'll not only do good for yourself, but for others as well. It's not selfish to pray for more joy. Your friends and family will be glad you did. Taking care of one's own mental health is a way of showing love to others. Even though being cheerful is not always possible, it is something we ought to cultivate out of love for our families. If we keep ourselves miserable by ignoring recreation or time with God, we're not just being unfair to ourselves, but to others as well.

Joy is a social virtue. A more genial spirit will produce more pleasant words. "Pleasant words are a honeycomb, sweet to the soul and healing to the bones" (16:24). The

Hebrew indicates that these "pleasant words" are motivated by love, not anger or evil intent. They breathe love, not only to restore but to preserve and advance health (Delitzsch, *Biblical Commentary on the Proverbs,* p. 348).

Though the Bible commends cheerfulness, it does not condemn depression. We are to permit each other some bad moods from time to time. Depression is sometimes a healing process, a proper part of grief over a lost job or loved one. Some periods of depression are quite serious and may require a year or two to overcome. We must be careful not to inflict guilt on ourselves and our partners during bouts with sadness.

There is a danger in reading a chapter like this; it's more easily applied to our partners than to ourselves. The picture of the ideal man and woman is not for judgment, but improvement. God's Word is a mirror to hold up to ourselves, not our mates. When we find a fault in ourselves, we are to correct it. Any flaw it shows in our mates we are to overlook. Noting Proverbs 10:12, Peter writes: "Above all, love each other deeply, because love covers over a multitude of sins" (1 Peter 4:8). The foundation of good marriages is not perfection, but forgiveness.

Chapter
SEVEN

INTIMACY: CLOSE UP

The intimate friend.
PROVERBS 2:17

At my marriage seminars I often ask participants to write down one word or a brief phrase to describe marriage. Then I invite them to share what they wrote down with their spouses. Some show their frustration, like the man who wrote, "God's idea. Don't ask me." Less than half the people come close to having the same ideas as their spouses, and rarely does a couple use the same word, which is understandable since marriage consists of many things. In our previous chapters, we've touched on a number of them: commitment, love, faithfulness to duties, and sex.

What word would you jot down to describe marriage? Jesus quoted Genesis 2:24 when portraying marriage: "For this reason a man will leave his father and mother and be united to his wife, and they will become one flesh." The biblical phrase for marriage is "one flesh." Though "one flesh" may include more than one ingredient of marriage, I have been contending for many years that the basic meaning is "intimacy." Marriage is unique because it is to be the closest of all relationships. We are not just committed to someone, but to something—being intimate.

Some writers prefer the word *companionship*. "Eve is a companion for Adam, created for him to overcome his one deficiency: 'it is not good for the man to be alone.' The reason for marriage is to solve the problem of loneliness," says one author (Jay Adams, *Marriage, Divorce and Remarriage in the Bible,* Presbyterian and Reformed Publishing Company, 1980, p. 8).

One writer has fiercely objected to this view, writing, "God did say, 'It is not good for the man to be alone,' but the *reason* He gave was that Adam needed a helper. God could have given Adam a *dog* if all Adam needed was a companion. God could have given Adam *another man* if companionship was all Adam needed." She argues: "Adam was not drooping about, overcome with loneliness, yearning for a companion. How could he be lonely, face to face with God? Adam was incomplete, not lonely. He needed a *helper.* He needed a woman" (Mary Pride, *The Way Home,* Crossroads Publishing, p. 16). Eve was created, she says, because Adam needed someone to be a mother to his children, making the birthing of children the primary purpose and nature of marriage.

Bible scholars throughout history would not agree with Mary Pride's interpretation. Being alone, Adam was incomplete; though he had intimate fellowship with God, he needed a close relationship with another person like himself. God had built into him a need for intimacy. Says the reformer John Calvin, "Solitude is not good. The combination of husband and wife in body and soul is intended to help man overcome his aloneness" (*Commentary on the Book of Genesis,* Wm. B. Eerdmans Publishing Company, vol. I, p. 128). One of the most prominent Old Testament specialists of the last century wrote, "The woman is to be Adam's helper and at the same time provide a companion, able to interchange thoroughly with him, and being in other respects his intellectual equal." In 1906 he wrote, "To become one flesh means the attachment between them becoming greater, and the union closer, even than that between parent and child" (S.R. Driver, *The Book of Genesis,* Methuen & Co., 1906, pp. 40-44).

We have good cause for understanding "one flesh" to

stand for intimacy. The word "flesh" in Hebrew can refer to the whole person, not just the body, making the "oneness" broader than the sexual relationship. Also the fact that God compares His relationship to Israel with the relationship between a husband and wife supports the idea that marriage is a close companionship. In other Scripture, marriage is pictured in this way. In the Song of Songs the wife is the husband's "darling" and "beautiful one" (2:10). He is the wife's "lover" and "friend" (5:16).

When all these bits of biblical evidence are put together, we have a strong case for associating intimacy with marriage. But a colleague of mine added a clincher to the arguments when he and I were teaching a course together. He pointed out that the word translated *partner* in Proverbs 2:17 really means "intimate friend," and it appears that way in Proverbs 16:28 and 17:9. "Intimate friends" may be the closest in meaning to "one flesh" in the Bible.

Naked with No Shame

The word *intimacy* gives us a good description of marriage because it includes the unique aspects of marriage. Intimacy, for example, is a primary ingredient of love. People in love share their secrets. As the revealing grows, so does the love. Cautiously, a young man says to his lover, "I am going to tell you something I've never told anyone else before." Eyes uplifted in anticipation, heart pounding with desire, her love for him expands with every secret from his lips.

"Love," says Erich Fromm, "is the act of penetration of the other person." In intimacy, one person lets another into his or her life. It is symbolized by the sexual union: as a wife freely allows her husband into the private depths of her body, she also permits him into her soul. As a couple, they are freely exposed to one another. Perhaps the description of the first couple, Adam and Eve, includes this broader intimacy: "The man and his wife were both naked, and they felt no shame" (Gen. 2:25). That sexual intercourse is described as "to know" in the Hebrew may be further evidence that love, sex, and intimacy are bound together. Broader than sex, intimacy requires a nakedness far more threatening than the taking off of one's clothes before another. Certain thoughts and feelings are difficult to share. Our hunger for intimacy may even be greater than our passion for sex. These two needs are sometimes hard to distinguish from one another. A counselor told us how one of his clients demonstrated that sexual feelings mingle with the desire for closeness. A single Christian woman came to him filled with shame and guilt by her impulsive affairs. Seemingly unable to control herself, she seduced salesmen and other strangers into her bed whenever they came to her door. The counselor finally explained to her that her obsession for sex was a deep yearning for intimacy. "Can you ask three friends to pledge to give you a hug every day?" he asked her. Though she could ask men for sex, she was embarrassed to ask friends for hugs. "I could never do that," she replied. "But I could give three hugs a day." Taking his advice, she daily embraced others and got warm affection back. As she did, her compulsion to seduce men vanished. The fact that this treatment actually worked for her confirms that we often lust for sex because we badly need to be close to someone.

Indoor Hide-and-Seek

Despite our great need for intimacy, I find persons in my seminars who say they have never thought of marriage in these terms. Often couples will say that they have very little intimacy. Perhaps our problem is that we are able to have sex without intimacy easier than we are able to have intimacy without sex. We have allowed the passion for another's body to replace the passion for another's soul. The lack of that passion is disturbing the domestic peace.

Today's wives are angry, vexed, and confused, claims a psychiatrist in a book called *Passive Men, Wild Women*. Women have gone wild over what's happening—or what's not happening—in their homes. He claims that the problem is universal, troublesome, and obvious. The enraged women who storm into his office all relate the same drama.

The husband arrives home around 7 o'clock exhausted from his day at work. He has spent the day dealing with people and their problems. He has had it up to his eyeballs. He wants to hide from everyone—including (especially?) his family. Silently he reads the paper and wolfs his dinner down. He pays only token attention to his wife, maybe a little more (or less) to the kids, and then withdraws behind TV's Monday night football or Tuesday night movie. Remaining semiglued to the television set through the 11 o'clock news, he eventually comes to bed with his wife, who is usually already asleep.

While women's stories vary, the plot's the same, and so is the problem. These wives want something more from their marriages. But her demands for longer talks, honest expressions of feelings, more time with the kids or her, help with domestic chores, or better sex all add up to one thing for him: pressure. More of that he doesn't need. He withdraws, retreats, and lapses into sullen silence. He gets more passive as his wife gets more hysterical. And eventually, often after years of this self-defeating pattern, she arrives in the psychiatrist's office (Pierre Mornell, Ballantine Books, pp. 1–3).

Overcoming Fish-Bowl Phobia

Time and pressure aren't the only barriers to intimacy. We avoid intimacy because we are afraid of it. Fear of being rejected is the biggest obstacle to intimacy. This is especially true in the beginning of a relationship. We expose ourselves slowly, since every secret we tell is like taking off a piece of armor. We want to be sure we are with a friend, with someone who loves us and will not be offended by what we really are.

If we fear sharing our real selves after years of marriage, it may be because we have been wounded by our spouse.

Sometimes a husband or wife will use the intimate knowledge against the partner. "I once told my husband I felt insecure," a woman told me. "Ever since then, in certain arguments, he will throw it back at me. 'You're just insecure,' he'll accuse. I wish I'd never told him." Intimacy is risky business. It will thrive only in a warm, accepting atmosphere.

Sometimes shame keeps us from exposing ourselves. At times, it's quite normal to be ashamed. All of us have strange feelings and thoughts we aren't proud of. If we tell about our sexual fantasies or weird feelings, we're afraid we'll be laughed at or disliked. But as a husband and wife become more comfortable with each other, they will be able to share more and more of the silly, sensitive, private thoughts. When they do, they will feel more loved and accepted because they will be appreciated for what they really are, not what their spouse thought they were. Ginger and I have revealed things we never thought we would, but only after years of closeness.

Shame is sometimes completely uncalled-for. We are needlessly embarrassed simply because we are critical of normal human emotions. We feel badly that we get angry, depressed, jealous, suspicious, or disappointed, and we hesitate to admit to those feelings. But there's nothing inherently wrong with these feelings. In certain situations it's OK to be angry or jealous. At times, even God is jealous. Distorted ideals make us reject ourselves and others, sometimes our spouses. In the early years of our marriage, Ginger was afraid to tell me about her periodic depression. Always a lighthearted person, she had a tiny bout with the blues during a certain time each month, part of the emotional fluctuation of her menstrual cycle. As a young wife, she hid behind a happy mask, too ashamed to admit she was in an emotional cellar, making her feel distant from me and lonely. Eventually she got the courage to let me know what was happening. She recalls the day she came to me and said, "Chick, I am really feeling down." Thankfully, I didn't condemn her or quote Scripture about rejoicing in the Lord. Instead, I simply said,

"Here's a shoulder to cry on." That day our marital intimacy took a leap forward.

To be open to each other, we must accept the whole range of human emotions, learning to accept ourselves as we are. If you are embarrassed to stand naked in front of a mirror, you will not feel good being exposed to your spouse. What is true of physical disrobing is also true of emotional unveiling. If you're not able to accept your inner self, you'll have a hard time sharing it with others. To be intimate, we need to come to grips with who we really are and learn to forgive and accept what we find. Then we won't have to hide behind a dishonest mask.

Because the reasons for our fears may lie in the forgotten past, we aren't always able to explain why we fear intimacy. Maybe our parents bombarded us with phrases like, "don't cry" and "don't feel sad," binding our emotions in a straitjacket of guilt. Even one major experience of rejection can close a person up tighter than a clam. Flashbacks of hurt, guilt, or shame can block self-exposure when you get close to it. Our relationships to God can help us deal with these things, His forgiveness enabling us to accept ourselves. But this will take time. From infancy our consciences were built by the words and events in our lives. The conscience can become distorted, making a person feel bad about doing good and good about doing bad. It is not always a reliable guide; it must be conformed to what is biblical. But the conscience is as stubborn to give up its feelings, formed bit by bit, as the body is to give up excess weight, added bite by bite. To shed weight, we diet and wait. To change our consciences we need the same kind of patience. We must keep on thinking the right things until we feel them, continually reminding ourselves of God's acceptance until we feel accepted. If excessive guilt and shame continue to block our intimacy, we will need to see a counselor for help. Our partners' approval will also help us become more intimate. It's a beautiful cycle: acceptance breeds intimacy, which breeds acceptance.

Yet another fear can make intimacy hard to achieve: the fear of being controlled. Self-revelation is a threat to some people because they fear losing themselves to another person. When we reveal ourselves to our lovers, we are, in a sense, being "taken" by them. The more we are known, the more we are possessed. Solomon's sweetheart says, "I am my lover's and my lover is mine" (Song 6:3). Being possessed frightens people for different reasons. Sometimes they are extremely individualistic, with personal goals and ambitions that a close relationship may make hard to achieve. Or they are very insecure. Such persons aren't really sure who they are. Inferiority feelings can also make someone afraid of intimacy. Thinking to himself, *I'm not worthy of her,* a husband keeps his genuine self locked up in a protective layer of silence.

Whether caused by feelings of inferiority or insecurity, this fear of losing one's self in marriage can be overcome. We will have to trust each other. As trust increases, so does intimacy. Honesty should come easily to Christians. Of all people, we should have nothing to hide; we admit our sinfulness. The church is the only group with public confession of sinfulness as a requirement for membership. If later we church members tell the truth that we harbor angry feelings at times, envy others, and think ugly thoughts, other members shouldn't be surprised. They know we are sinners because we told them when we joined. If we do as Scripture tells us and accept one another as Christ accepted us, we will create a climate for intimacy (Rom. 15:7). We should not tear off each other's masks, like a husband brutally stripping a shy bride of her clothes. Rather, we will try to foster a climate of warm acceptance that will enable our lovers to slowly open to us as the petals of a rose unfold in the sunlight.

A man and wife should passionately want to know each other. One man said it well: "I see my wife as a vast forest, and I'm an explorer." If the searching stops, the excitement stops, and marriage becomes a bore. There are some effective guidelines for opening ourselves and our marriages to the thrilling potentials of intimacy.

Marriage Is Close Work
Take your time. Self-disclosure is best when it's gradual. Intimacy doesn't require telling everything, and certainly not telling it too quickly. Some of the wonder of love is the mystery of the one loved. The secrets we hold, as well as the ones we tell, contribute to the vitality of our relationship.

Erik Erikson, prominent expert on human development, marks young adulthood as the period when intimacy needs to be learned. Intimacy includes the ability to be committed to close and lasting relationships and the willingness to sacrifice and compromise as those relationships require (*Childhood and Society,* Norton, p. 163). Young adulthood stretches from the years after age 18 to age 39. Learning the art of intimacy may take many years. The search to know each other will last a lifetime.

See clearly the many forms of intimacy. Intimacy is like a city with scores of highways leading to it. Perhaps the most profound intimacy comes from peering deeply into the inner caverns of another person's soul. Call that *communication intimacy,* made up of the telling of secrets, sharing of personal emotions, and disclosure of visions, hopes, and plans. This kind of intimacy may surpass *physical intimacy:* the touch of each other's bodies, the color of her eyes, the sound of his voice. Another road to intimacy is *emotional:* making each other laugh, standing near while one of you cries, being bored or depressed together. Sickness, as many couples will testify, can make a husband and wife feel very close. The ailing partner speaks honestly of aches and pains; the nursing mate shows loving concern and care. Even hard times can draw us emotionally near. *Intellectual intimacy* offers great rewards: discussing a book you both read, sharing your concept of God, arguing about politics, discussing new ideas. Then, there's *social intimacy:* liking the same people, having a long talk with another couple, meeting with a small group, or enjoying a party. Intimacy has a *spiritual* form: worshiping with other Christians, praying as a couple, studying God's Word, talking of your faith and doubts. *Recreation* together affords intimate opportunities: winning a game or losing one, bird-watching, hiking, camping, and countless other activities. *Creating and serving* can be intimate: redecorating the bedroom, refinishing a chair, helping with a local fund drive, team teaching a Sunday School class, ministering to the poor.

Intimacy is like a diamond, with many facets. If a couple recognizes this, they can more easily cultivate what is most satisfying and easy for them. Couples, for example, who can't pray together because of differences in belief about God can still enjoy other forms of closeness. A marriage can thrive on any type of intimacy. Some couples may have little sexual intimacy but be very close in other ways.

All couples can see that sex is only one form of intimacy to enjoy. They will even learn to enjoy physical closeness without sex. Holding hands, sitting close together, kissing, and hugging can be very satisfying even when they don't lead to the bedroom. Both husbands and wives need these types of intimacy more than they realize. It's a well-known fact that many women enjoy the activities that lead to sexual intercourse more than they do the act itself. But men too may really want the closeness even more than the pleasure that sex brings them. One anthropologist maintains that men want sex because they want to be held. In our culture, there aren't many acceptable ways for them to be hugged; they want sex because they want sensual closeness.

Show appreciation for what intimacies your partner gives. While a couple works at cultivating more types of intimacy, they can also value the intimacy they already have. Perhaps a husband doesn't put his feelings into words; but he may be exposing his emotions to his wife through a carefully selected anniversary card, a poem cut from a magazine, or a surprise gift. If a wife misses these messages, pressuring him to say words that are hard for him to say, she will frustrate rather than foster his attempts at intimacy.

Both husband and wife can learn to appreciate the little but potent intimacies: a warm glance, a hand on the shoulder, a knowing smile, and lingering smells, tastes, and memories of each other. A friend of mine tells me that playing tennis with his wife is a very intimate experience. "Across the net, without saying a word, we exchange all kinds of thoughts and feelings through the faces we make and the casual glances we give. If someone were watching us," he says, "they would have no idea that all of that was going on between us."

Although intimacy is bound up in activities, it is primarily a feeling. We can say of intimacy what we say of camp fires: "each one is warmed by the memory of a thousand previous camp fires." Intimacy is the feeling of closeness derived from the myriads of previous close encounters.

Develop intimate communication. Words build bridges between people. Without language, there would be little companionship. Helen Keller learned in a dramatic way how communication and friendship are tied together. Deaf and blind as a child, she acted like a frightened animal, isolated in her dark and silent world. Her desperate parents hired a tutor, Anne Sullivan, to deal with the little girl whom many people had labeled an idiot. For weeks Anne spelled words into Helen's little palm, trying to make her understand a symbol for things like "cup" and "water." More than sixty years later, Helen Keller recorded her own recollections of what it was like when her tutor finally broke through to her world.

> It happened at the well-house, where I was holding a mug under a spout. Annie pumped water into it, and when the water gushed out into my hand she kept spelling w-a-t-e-r into my other hand with her fingers. Suddenly, I understood. Caught up in the first joy I had known since my illness, I reached out eagerly to Annie's ever-ready hand, begging for new words to identify whatever objects I

touched. Spark after spark of meaning flew from hand to hand and, miraculously, affection was born. From the wellhouse there walked two enraptured beings calling each other 'Helen' and 'Teacher.' (in Alan Loy McGinnis, *The Friendship Factor,* Augsburg Publishing House, pp. 60-61)

With all of the senses intact, many couples know little of this rapture of being close. They feel isolated, though they live in the same home. Married, they are emotionally divorced.

There are practical things husbands and wives can do to help themselves put into words what they feel. One counselor tells couples to start by "sharing your scare." In other words, talk about why it's hard for you to talk. When you do that, you are not only helping your mate understand you, but you are actually doing what is hard for you: verbalizing your feelings.

Responding properly to your partner's expression of feelings is crucial to helping them open up. People are like the groundhogs in our area: when they stick their heads out of their holes and sense the slightest bit of hostility, they quickly pop back inside. Married people won't expose themselves to one another if they are criticized or laughed at whenever they do. Nor will they if they are ignored, which is something that seems to happen a lot. I often hear, "I don't share my feelings because my husband simply doesn't care how I feel." Even when a person's partner responds well, it is still difficult for some couples to speak of intimate things. They can help each other if they put themselves into situations that call for more intimacy. Watch an emotional TV show and then talk about it over a cup of hot chocolate. Read a page or two from a book together and then ask, "How does it make you feel?" After a worship service, talk about what you thought or felt about the sermon subject or the hymns.

Besides the things we do together, the experiences we have alone can contribute to our closeness, as we talk about them afterward. If we are always together, we may have less to tell each other. Even separate vacations now and then may give us each something stimulating to share, as we report not only the events, but our feelings and reactions.

Be patient. A word of caution: we should not be too eager to learn too much, too fast. A loving relationship consists of what you don't know as well as what you do know about each other. Kept secrets contribute to a relationship just as revealed ones do. There is a mysterious side of love. What is hidden creates a feeling of wonderment. Even the most intimate of couples will not be completely known to each other.

Being intimate is more exciting than it is simple. Andrew Greeley observes that "intimacy is always difficult and when it stops being difficult, it stops being intimate" (*Love and Play,* Thomas More Press, 1975, p. 64). Through years of persistent, patient unfolding, a couple can create a relationship that deserves the title "intimate friends."

Chapter
EIGHT

SENSUAL IS SAGE

Drink water from your own cistern.
PROVERBS 5:15

"Sex is such a bother; wouldn't we be better off without it?" In one of my seminar sessions, a woman raised this question. It's not hard to understand her thinking; sex is a hassle to most of us, a terrible bother to one out of two married couples, according to one "sexpert." If you are tempted to skip this chapter you are not alone. Sex in your marriage could be an annoyance that you would just as soon do without. Your lack of interest may be driving your spouse up the bedroom wall. Or maybe you're the one who is frustrated over trying to make lovemaking more satisfying.

There's a lot of personal anguish over sex. Lustful thoughts crowd out whatever is true, lovely, right. Sex can turn love to improper lust, pleasant daydreams to corrupt fantasies. Within us are the "sinful desires, which war against our souls" (1 Peter 2:11). There are also the ugly sexual crimes: child pornography, rape, incest, and so on.

We can see why someone would ask, "why bother?" In fact great sex is not always necessary for a satisfactory marriage. So the question makes sense: are the pleasures of sex equal to the pain it causes? Thankfully, we don't have to answer that question, since sex is part of life, whether we like it or not.

If the sexual side of marriage troubles you, this chapter

could help. If your lovemaking is fine, this chapter could be a step toward making it better. Not all sexual difficulties are that hard to cope with. Lack of information or wrong attitudes cause most of them. Knowing what the Bible says about it can help with this. Surveys show that religious women have better sex lives than nonreligious ones. They feel sex is OK because God created it. This proper frame of mind is what husbands and wives most need between their bedsheets. But information may not be enough for persons whose attitudes and feelings are so deeply embedded that they need a trained counselor to help them change them.

A Good Kind of Intoxication

On the subject of sex, Proverbs has a major passage. "Drink water from your own cistern, running water from your own well," the wise man tells the husband (5:15). He leaves no doubt that he is referring to the wife's sexual charms. "May your fountain be blessed, and may you rejoice in the wife of your youth. A loving doe, a graceful deer—may her breasts satisfy you always, may you ever be captivated by her love" (5:18-19).

Some people have a hard time believing sex should be enjoyable, let alone captivating. I never speak on the subject without some Christian telling me that he or she can't have sex without guilt. Just last month a woman said, "After forty years of marriage, I think that after listening to your talk, I have shed my guilt feelings about sex." The Apostle Paul warns about false prophets that forbid marriage. They will have consciences that are seared with a hot branding iron (1 Tim. 4:2-3). In the deep inner self, they have been stamped with the wrong concept: "sex is dirty." Their consciences are like computers that have been wrongly programmed. Instead of listening to their branded consciences, they must reprogram them. For some, that will take a great deal of time.

Programming the conscience begins very early in life. The

way a mother nurses a baby plays a part in whether that baby will grow up to enjoy sex or shrink from it. Sexual abuse can create troubling attitudes. A woman told me she could not have intercourse with her husband without severe pain. Doctors told her the problem was in her mind, not her body. As she related stories from her childhood, I could see why. Her grandfather had been the first to violate her, exposing himself in the cab of his truck, ordering her to play sexual games when she was only four years old. In her early teens another relative had repeatedly forced himself on her. Embarrassed and afraid to tell her parents, she stored the disgust in the basement of her mind where, like rotting fruit, the stench of it spread throughout her soul. Being a Christian, she was aware of Christ's forgiveness, acceptance, and cleansing. But the cleansing of her conscience would take time and effort.

Most of us have wounded consciences in regard to sex. Some don't feel guilty when they should, others do when they should not. Conscience is not a reliable guide. It must be shaped and reshaped continually throughout a lifetime. The blueprint for remodeling the conscience is Scripture. Scripture says that sex with the right person, at the right time, and in the right place is one of God's greatest blessings. This is not a new idea bred in our modern sensuous society. For centuries, biblical scholars have taught this. "Conjugal love is first among earthly blessings that God in mercy gives us. . . . Enjoy then with thankfulness what's yours," wrote Charles Bridges over one hundred years ago in his commentary on Proverbs (George F. Santa, *A Modern Study in the Book of Proverbs: Charles Bridges' Classic Revised for Today's Readers,* Mott Media, 1978, p. 70).

Satisfying the Sexual Thirst at Home
Satisfying sex in marriage will prevent sinful sex outside it. Using the same word three times, Proverbs 5:15-23 has a unique way of explaining this. First, the husband is told to

"be captured" by his wife's love. Then, he is told not to "be captured" by an adulteress. If so, he will have been "led astray" by his folly. The meaning is this: the way to avoid being led astray by an adulteress, and thus being captured by foolishness, is to be taken captive by your wife's love.

The husband should "drink water" from his own cistern, meaning satisfy his sexual appetite at home. Why quench thirst at a neighbor's well when you have one of your own? Also, a husband should not allow his springs to overflow in the streets. This might refer to a man's sexual passion or his fathering illegitimate children. No doubt, even the command to rejoice in his wife includes having children by her as well as sex with her. Ignoring a wife for other women is like wasting precious water; it makes no sense.

The New Testament also teaches that sex in marriage will prevent sex outside of it. In 1 Corinthians, Paul advises: "But, since there is so much immorality . . . the husband should fulfill his marital duty to his wife, and likewise the wife to her husband" (7:2-3). Because Paul's disciples were surrounded by prostitution, some of it in the pagan worship services, he advises them to get married to satisfy their sexual lust. To married couples, he further explains, "The wife's body does not belong to her alone, but also to her husband. In the same way, the husband's body does not belong to him alone but also to his wife" (7:4). In marriage, sex is an obligation, not an option. I meet scores of Christians who have battled with temptation and fantasies for years because their spouses have little or no interest in satisfying their sexual needs. Satisfying each other's sexual needs is so crucial that Paul writes, "Do not deprive one another except by mutual consent and for a time, so that you may devote yourselves to prayer. Then come together again so that Satan will not tempt you because of your lack of self-control" (7:5). Not even fasting and prayer should be used for an excuse for giving up sex. Abstaining too long will give Satan a chance to entice you to sin. Research tells us that those who get into sex outside their marriages are those who had little inside their marriages. Marital security is linked to good marital sex. Keeping sex extra special can keep it from being extramarital.

Creative Conception

Sex in marriage is also good because through it a couple participates in God's creative activity. Sexual yearnings are tied into our deep desire to be productive and creative. Through the birth of their child, a man and woman make a contribution to the world. Passion's fruit is not merely immediate gratification; it can also produce a new life. This is the Creator's way of making persons in His image; how can it be a degrading, dirty act? In the passions of the marriage bed, God, the artist, is creating His masterpiece, man. Granted, not every sexual act produces a child. There is more to sex than that. Still, making children validates making love.

Conception demands that couples be stripped of their normal dignity and lose themselves in passion. This bothers some people, like the wife of a friend of mine. "I hate all of that acting like an animal," she said. Besides insulting animals, this woman was not being very kind to herself or her husband. Nowhere does the Bible accuse humans of acting like animals. The sounds and movements of lovemaking are human. Just because animals may do some of the same things does not turn humans into animals. Sex was not corrupting this woman; her attitudes were corrupting sex.

In certain periods of history, this dim view of sex prevailed. Martin Luther quoted doctors in his time who compared orgasms to epileptic fits. But God sanctified sex by making it His method for creating people.

Having a baby is a fruit of a couple's love for one another. Their loving union is now made concrete in a child, composed of both of them. Being a product of his parents' love can make a child feel secure and special. When parents divorce, a child may wonder why the love that brought him or her into the world was not strong enough to keep them together. One young man told of the deep pain he felt when his recently divorced father said, "I never loved your mother; I never should have married her." Shocked, the boy replied, "And does that mean that I should never have been born?"

Waiting for conception, a couple senses the mystery and privilege in their sexual embrace, not knowing which of these special times will be used by the Creator. Even after all their children are born, a special flavor can permeate their lovemaking because they know that their sex life has produced life. The delight, fulfillment, and joy of having children beautify (if we will allow them to) the act of ejaculation and orgasm, the odor of semen and glands. Conception and birth should purify sex in our minds. Perhaps this is why older couples make the best sex partners. Shame and disgrace, if they ever had any, have disappeared, leaving them more comfortable with each other's sensuality.

Intimate Sex

The sex life of a husband and wife is also made beautiful by what it means to them. Sex includes the soul as well as the body. Biblical sex is not just a matter of glands and hormones. In Hebrew the verb for having sexual intercourse is "to know," tying together sex and intimacy. Much of the thrill of sex is the joy of intimacy. Touching, interlocking our secret selves, we sense the mystery of the marital embrace. We hear, see, and feel each other in ways no other person can. This satisfies the deep need we have to be close.

This is the essence of the magnetism between the sexes. Passion compels each to clutch and lunge in a desperate attempt to be "one flesh." The actual physical interlocking symbolizes the personal merging. We yearn to penetrate and be penetrated to fulfill our emotional and social need to connect.

The unselfish giving in sex also glorifies it. Jesus' words "It is more blessed to give than to receive" (Acts 20:35) apply to the physical. Studies show that people who like to give pleasure to their partners take more delight in sex. But of course, sex wonderfully includes both the giving and receiving. In it is the essence of romantic love; one person is giving to another, but receiving at the same time. At other times, sex can be sacrificial: the partner gives himself to the other even though not in the mood to be aroused. Yet, there is pleasure or satisfaction in that kind of giving for those who love each other.

In recent centuries it was felt that the woman received her sexual satisfaction from giving. She took pleasure in delighting the male who was the only one who would really enjoy sex. But from the biblical point of view, both husband and wife have needs for sexual pleasure and release. In the New Testament Paul makes this clear: not only does the woman belong to the man, but the woman has authority over the husband's body. To spare her greater temptation, her needs must be satisfied. While the Proverbs stress the man's delight in his wife, other Old Testament passages view sex as appetizing for the woman as well. Her lover is like an "apple tree"; she says, "His fruit is sweet to my taste" (Song 2:3). God built the woman's body for her own pleasure as well as that of her husband. "The woman's clitoris contributes nothing to having babies; it is only there for a woman's pleasure," a physician told me. This means that it is proper for a man to help his wife find pleasure and release at times when he has no need for sex. He can find ways to bring her to a climax when she has a need.

Letting Go

Sexual relating in marriage symbolizes belongingness in marriage. The Song of Songs states it poetically: "I am my lover's and my lover is mine" (6:3). The sense of completion that each feels in being part of a one-flesh relationship creates a sense of ownership. That belongingness reaches a high point in the sexual embrace. This may cause us to value and demand absolute abandonment. We want our lover to hold back nothing, to be "all there." Perhaps, this is one of the sources of sexual problems, since some people dread this loss of self. Some women do not have orgasms because they can't let go of themselves. If a person has trouble being "owned," he or she may have trouble being interested in sex or in reaching a climax.

Almost always, our problems with sex are problems of the personality. Sex is tied into our capacity to love, to be intimate, to give, to receive, to lose ourselves in another. Personality flaws show up in sexual deviation. Without love, the rapist uses sex to dominate, hurt, and control; the sadistic person, without sensitivity, finds pleasure in hurting. Sex for them is a way of acting out their distorted emotional, mental selves. The good lover acts out his maturity.

Sex begins in the head, not in the bed. We use sex to say things to each other. If we have nothing to say to our partners, we hear only buzzing. Like the eagle, which symbolizes liberty to the citizens of the United States, sex symbolizes many things to the marital relationship. If our country had no freedom, the eagle atop its flagpole would be a sham. When intimacy, sacrificial giving, and abandonment are absent from a marriage, sex in bed is an empty biological act.

Our greatest sexual sin comes from emptying it of its true meaning. Adultery denies the intimacy and belongingness of sex. One has no business physically joining with a stranger, with whom one has no commitment or closeness. Married persons can have this same problem if they have a physical relationship without a personal one. Not that they should stop having sex, since they owe that to each other. But they should enrich the rest of their relationship. Sex is an act of body and soul. When the aroused body takes part while the soul looks on in indifference, sex becomes a lie. No wonder a partner can feel betrayed and used, like the woman who said, "The only time my husband says he loves me is during sexual intercourse."

Drink Your Fill, Lovers

Intimacy puts the sizzle into sex. Enriching physical intimacy requires increasing personal intimacy. This doesn't mean that every time a couple has sex it has to be a profound personal encounter. For physical release or just plain fun, the so called "quickies" are OK. But better sex comes from a better relationship. A couple needs quality time together. Couples with young children are among the first to report that the bedroom has become the dull room. When children come into the home, romance can easily go out. Leisurely evenings in front of the stereo give way to trips to the playground. Late nights once spent in each other's arms are now consumed by comforting a sick or restless child. Without intimate times together, their lovemaking is reduced to quick meetings of the bodies and not the souls. They need more walks, more candlelight dinners, more romance. Priority must be given to sharing their feelings, writing love notes, treating each other to breakfast in bed, checking into a motel for a weekend.

Combining sexual activities with intimate ones can also increase the intimate messages of sensuality. Listening to romantic music might increase the feeling of love. Reading love poems or notes you've written to each other while sitting partially nude in bed can increase the feeling of closeness. Sexual technique can play a part. Just as the growing relationship makes the sex life better, richer sex can enrich the total relationship. The meaning of sex and the practice of sex are very closely tied together. Making sex more colorful will make it communicate more. Granted, it's a mistake to have new technique without feeling; but it's just as bad to have feeling without technique. New positions of sexual intercourse and creative ways of using your mouth and hands don't just increase pleasure. Technique and meaning are bound together. It's no secret that the most ordinary position for intercourse with the man on top symbolizes the man's aggressiveness and the woman's submission. For this reason some men feel threatened if the wife wants to reverse their positions. Men who feel superior to women, or who think they must always be in charge may find lying on their backs during intercourse a very uncomfortable thing. Some women, too, may find the bottom place better because they are turned on by the man's dominating them.

Freedom to Create

Sex becomes a sort of art form whenever the couple creatively tries to send a message through the method. As artists fashion exquisite creations from pieces of driftwood, bits of yarn, or matchsticks, couples create rapturous collages of intimacy out of nothing but themselves.

This artistry requires releasing the child in us. We become like the little child who brings the dandelion to his mother; he is really bringing himself—his innocent love. As the child delights in running through a field, we delight in running our fingers through each other's hair. We are searching for simple childlike ways of saying I love you, want you, adore you. The beauty of sex is in its nakedness. Not just the exposure of our private selves, but rather the absence of clothes—or of anything whatsoever. Entered into properly, it is an affront to materialism that insists we must buy, use, or own something to enjoy. For thrilling sex we need nothing—in fact we shed everything. This is why sex not only makes us take off, but shut out. We have no one but each other and need only each other—and God—for these enchanting moments. And having Him there makes it even more remarkable because we know our passion is bred by His passion for us.

Good sex manuals can teach a couple the art of lovemaking and make them more willing to experiment. To try new things the husband and wife must see the profound possibilities in the rather profane instructions. Mechanical directions like "put your leg here" or "place your hand there" embarrass some readers. But they will discover that trying new things will yield wonders. In the side-by-side position, for instance, they may feel more like intimate friends, lying together, in prolonged union, leisurely pleasuring one another with slow movements, and deep eye contact. They may not like all the things they try. Different approaches will lead to new experiments. Much of a couple's creativity will occur spontaneously during the heat of passion, as long as each is willing to cooperate with the other's mundane requests to raise a leg or move to another position.

The creative couple will proclaim liberty in their bedroom, doing whatever they wish so long as they don't harm or force one another. In a marriage, each will slowly open up to the other, as the petals of a rose unfold. Feelings of guilt will fade as the years of loving close encounters mount up.

Spontaneous expressions of love should not be hindered by unnecessary rules about what positions or practices are right or wrong between two lovers. If it increases the pleasure and intimacy between them, it's right. Being uptight about what a couple does in the bedroom only makes their marriage worse.

Proverbs also makes it clear that we should not be reluctant to enjoy the pleasures of sex. "May her breasts satisfy you always, may you ever be captivated by her love" (5:19). Being captivated is like being intoxicated. It is not wrong to be carried away by sensual pleasure.

God intended sex to be delicious. In the Song of Songs, the man says of his wife: "How beautiful you are and how pleasing, O love, with your delights! Your stature is like that of the palm, and your breasts like clusters of fruit" (7:6-7). She accents the pleasure of sex by comparing herself to a garden to which she invites him: "Let my lover come into his garden and taste its choice fruits" (4:16). Scripture often mixes images of drinking with sensuality. "You are a garden fountain, a well of flowing water streaming down from Lebanon" (Song of Songs 4:15). "Your love is more delightful than wine" (Song 1:2). "I have come into my garden, my sister, my bride.... I have drunk my wine and my milk. Eat, O friends, and drink; drink your fill, O lovers" (5:1).

Cultivating the Garden

To make marriage a sensual feast, we can put more novelty into sex in a number of ways.

First, cultivate your approach to lovemaking. A sensuous wife learns how to seduce her husband; a good man knows how to turn on his wife. Unfortunately, adulterers and adulteresses know more about seduction than married persons. Note the words of the temptress in Proverbs, as she borrows from the images from the Song of Songs:

> I have covered my bed with colored linen from Egypt.
> I have perfumed my bed with myrrh, aloes and cinnamon.
> Come, let's drink deep of love till morning; let's enjoy ourselves with love! (7:16-18).

Women can initiate romantic encounters with their husbands. In some respects they have the advantage over men, since it is easier to predict what will arouse a man than what will turn on a woman. What excites a woman one month may not even get her attention the next. The man is more like a padlock with a key. Unlocking his sensuality isn't too difficult once his wife has the key. But a woman is more like a complex combination lock that won't always open up with the same numbers.

Sights usually awaken a man's passion; words are more apt to arouse a wife. A compliment for her in the morning may make her desire him in the evening. Like the lover in the Song of Songs, he should praise her charms: "How beautiful you are, my darling" (Song 4:1). "How delightful is your love, my sister, my bride!" (4:10) Men too need affirmation. "How handsome you are, my lover! Oh, how charming," she says of him (1:16). If we look carefully we can see the beauty in each other, even when we are old. If husbands and wives are desirable to one another, it may have more to do with their standards of beauty than their wrinkles and flabs. Beauty lies in a person's character and sacrificial devotion. There are beautiful persons and handsome lovers that are far from a "ten" rating on Hollywood's scale of beauty. And there are number tens that are lousy lovers and unattractive persons. This limited physical standard of beauty often prevents husbands and wives from giving genuine compliments. Body size and shape have little to do with satisfying sex.

Besides words, women, especially, are turned on by touch. Not the grabbing sort of touching, but slow featherlike strokes or refreshing backrubs. Individuals are unique when it comes to what arouses them. One man told me that helping his wife with anything she is doing kindles her fire more than anything else. The combination to each other's lock is something you each will have to discover.

Another guideline is this: go slowly. Let agreement be the guide. Slowly expand your repertoire as you open up. Statistics show that wives don't reach their peak of sensuality until some time in their thirties. The husband eager to do new things must learn patience. Think of it as bringing her along on an adventure. The more she enjoys the first part of the trip, the more willing she will be to be led further. Her sensuality is like a garden locked up (Song 4:12). The layers of restraint will not always be removed quickly.

Another way to enrich your love life is to change the circumstances. Place is important to lovemaking. It is a well-known fact that staying in a motel turns on most people. A motel provides the basic essentials for great romantic love: privacy (alone to dress and undress as we like; the feeling that there's no one else in the world but us); freedom (to yell, moan, play, laugh, without the neighbors or kids hearing); uninterrupted time and space (no demanding doorbell or kids screaming for help); novelty (different colors, smells, feel of chairs and bed; distance away from daily concerns and cares). Compare that to a young wife's description of the scene of their lovemaking: "Our bedroom is small; we have wall-to-wall bed; there are no decorations; the skinny partitions don't prevent our neighbors from hearing any passionate squeal or bedspring squeak; while I'm on my back I keep looking up at the bare light bulb that hangs in the center of the ceiling." Her husband agreed with her description but could not understand why she said she felt "like a dirty prostitute in a cheap flophouse." After over an hour, we made some headway with him: he would get a light fixture to cover the bare bulb.

Do you need to do something about your environment for lovemaking? Privacy? Granted, if you have kids, you can't keep them from yelling out, but a lock on the door will prevent them from bursting in. Freedom? Drown out sounds with music. Send the kids to the sitter and have the house alone. Uninterrupted time and space? Schedule time so you can have a whole evening. Or novelty? Expensive hotels are not the only answer to this. How about another room in the house? Or out-of-doors, or a camp tent? In one of my seminars a woman volunteered that, though over forty years of age when it happened, she and her husband's most memorable lovemaking session took place on a lonely road in the back seat of their car. Why not?

Hordes of people in this world scoff or at least snicker at the advice of Proverbs that married couples can have great sex. Robust sex, for them, is outside of marriage. We can learn from a woman who recently said, "I have now learned that the best sex is with someone you love." Before saying that, she had written a best-selling paperback telling women that great sex was to be found in doing anything with any man anywhere. Through that book, *The Sensual Woman*, Joan Garrity had a major influence on American women. Now, after being a part of the sexual revolution of the sixties, she is a married woman, aware that truly satisfying sex can be found there after all. Had she consulted them, the Scriptures would have told her that. Sex outside of marriage is wrong, not simply because it's bad, but because sex in marriage is so good. We need to spread the word.

Chapter
NINE

IMPROVING YOUR CLASH ASSETS

> Every fool is quick to quarrel.
> PROVERBS 20:3

When the Voyager 2 spacecraft whipped past the planet Uranus, it sent back a description of the old planet that baffled scientists. They were astonished by the way the planet behaved in opposite ways to what they expected. "We're happily bewildered," said Edward Stone, major project scientist. "We'd be disappointed if we weren't bewildered because that's when you learn the most about new things," he said ("Uranus a Solar-System Misfit," *Chicago Tribune*, January 28, 1986, p. 1).

He's absolutely correct. Bewilderment is the prelude to learning, in outer space or in marriage. Unfortunately, most of us don't relish being befuddled over our partner's behavior as scientists do over a planet's. Just a few weeks after our wedding, Ginger and I plunged into a serious conflict between us. We didn't fight about it. Nor did we scream. But we were both feeling very hurt and very misunderstood. We were puzzled, disappointed, and sometimes inwardly angry with each other. The thing I most remember is how tough it was even to discuss it. It took several years before it was resolved. In the meantime, the conflict caused us to change, mature, and learn a great deal about each other and ourselves.

Conflict in the family can be a valuable commodity, though you might not think that at first when you read many of the Proverbs. They seem to caution us to avoid it. For example, "Starting a quarrel is like breaching a dam; so drop the matter before a dispute breaks out" (17:14). Or, take this one: "It is to a man's honor to avoid strife, but every fool is quick to quarrel" (20:3). It's plain: avoid strife.

Sweeping Conflict Under the Proverbial Rug

We have to be careful here. These verses aren't telling us to sweep our differences under the proverbial rug. *Strife* is a synonym for combat, not discussion. Most often it refers to physical battle, and very often, verbal scrimmages. It's the same Hebrew word translated "quarrel" in Proverbs 17:14. Strife and quarreling are responses to differences we have in our relationships. We are to shun the wrong response to discord, not the discord itself.

Making this distinction is crucial. People often fail to handle conflict wisely because they aren't willing to face it. This often stems from the attitude that conflict is wrong—that Christians shouldn't have it.

"Why do we have this problem?" she said. Her face displayed the same kind of bewilderment scientists felt when they looked at the pictures of Uranus. But she saw far more pain than hope in her experience. "We constantly differ over decisions. He wants to sell the extra refrigerator in the basement; I think we should keep it. I think we should paint the outside of the house this summer; he thinks next summer is best. What's wrong with us?" I surprised her and her husband a bit: "Not a thing," I said. "You look like two human beings to me, each with different temperaments and opinions. Conflict comes because you are trying to relate." Marriage is a merger. It's like the joining of two mountain streams with the bubbling, gurgling, rushing, foaming, and churning. It's dramatic. But of course it can also be trying, especially when the differences are great or crucial ones.

Even if you believe a wife should be submissive, there is still room for conflict. Remember that Abraham and Sarah had their differences, even though she was considered to be a model wife (1 Peter 3:5-6).

Not accepting conflict can cause several serious things to happen. First, you do what the woman I've been talking about did. You assume something's wrong—with one of you. You want to blame someone. If conflict is evil, one of you must be dreadful. Then something else can happen: disappointment sets in. "I'd hoped my marriage wasn't going to be like my mother's. I just can't stand our clashing the way they did." The couple's first disagreement is like finding a hair in the soup: "Oh, no, not this." Dismay comes into the marriage like a chilly drizzle on a cold autumn day. We become sullen and sulky. Or else our anger soars: we lash out, cry, argue, complain.

That's when the third dangerous thing happens: nothing. That is, couples just react without sensibly dealing with the problem. Instead of seeing the difference as an issue to be solved, they see it as an intruder that just ought to go away. It won't. Attempts to drive it out with blame, sarcasm, shouting, and physical violence are in vain.

The Book of Proverbs counsels us to avoid negative, sinful responses to conflict, not to avoid conflict. Though it tells us that love covers over all wrongs (10:12), it warns against not speaking up when you should: "Better is open rebuke than hidden love" (27:5). Loving includes rebuking.

A Good Earful Like a Gold Earring

Interpersonal discord is to be handled by bringing it up. It's profitable to show a person his fault. "He who rebukes a man will in the end gain more favor than he who has a flattering tongue" (Prov. 28:23). It is a great asset to have someone show you your wrong. A wise person will rate a good rebuke right up there with gold and silver: "A word aptly spoken is like apples of gold in settings of silver. Like an earring of gold or an ornament of fine gold is a wise man's rebuke to a listening ear" (25:11-12).

If a wise man's wife says, "You don't spend enough time with the family," he'll love it. If a husband tells a wise wife, "You're getting too busy to be the kind of companion I need," she will adore him for it. "Rebuke a wise man and he will love you" (9:8).

Some folks won't like being criticized. "Whoever corrects a mocker brings on insult; whoever rebukes a wicked man incurs abuse" (9:7). So watch out for the mocker and the wicked; they'll fight back if you try to give them a little friendly flak. The root problem of this scorner is lack of humility. The mocker is proud and haughty (21:24).

Perhaps it is the spirit of humility that lies at the basis of good relationships. The proud person hates rebuke because he is right in his own eyes. "The way of a fool seems right to him, but a wise man listens to advice" (12:15). "The proud and arrogant man—'Mocker' is his name; he behaves with overweening pride" (21:24). Though the mocker is a wicked, ungodly person, there is a lesson here for all of us. We should be willing both to receive and to give rebuke. We must be brave and humble enough to face up to conflict.

In other words, we must be open—open to what others think, feel, and have to say. Studies consistently show that open communication is necessary to good marital adjustment. One of the chief complaints of dissatisfied wives is that their husbands do not talk things over with them frequently enough. The happily married report that they do. It has been thought that couples can be too open, that if a spouse brings up his or her disappointments about the other it can lead to hurt and poor marital adjustment. There is some truth to that. We must be careful of being too harsh or too contentious. Our sharing must not be merely to get things off our chests, but to get them out in the open and settled. Some studies indicate that the biggest danger is in keeping too much in. Full disclosure of feelings tends to increase marital satisfaction (Bernard G. Guerney, Jr., et al., *Relationship*

Enhancement, Jossey-Bass Publishers, 1977, p. 196).

The Family Terrorist

Proverbs has lots of warnings and guidelines related to dealing with conflict. Let's begin with the most obvious: do not be a contentious person. This type of person is least able to negotiate conflicts. "A quarrelsome wife is like a constant dripping" (19:13). "Better to live on a corner of the roof than share a house with a quarrelsome wife" (25:24). The husband might also be the one who quibbles. "As charcoal to embers and as wood to fire, so is a quarrelsome man for kindling strife" (Prov. 26:21). A man can keep a marriage fired up too.

The wise man in Proverbs does not shrink from pointing out that some people are consistently bad. The quarrelsome wife is so uncontrollable that "restraining her is like restraining the wind or grasping oil with the hand" (27:16). She is almost impossible to live with.

A woman once admitted to me that the biggest problem in her marriage was her mouth. The couple's discord was created by her vocal cords. She knew this and struggled with it. Early in their marriage, she and her husband went for counsel to a pastor. The husband, who feared the pastor would side with his Christian wife, was delightfully surprised that he took his side. After an hour with them, he made the wife promise to read chapter three of James twice a day for a month. Was she angry when at home she found what he had asked her to read! "All kinds of animals, birds, reptiles and creatures of the sea are being tamed and have been tamed by man, but no man can tame the tongue. It is a restless evil, full of deadly poison" (James 3:7-8).

"When I found out what she was angry about," her husband told me, "I made an appointment with the pastor the next day and he led me to Christ. I had never been able to trust a minister before, but a man with that kind of courage and wisdom I would listen to."

If we are wise, we will use these proverbs to judge ourselves and not our mates. They are intended to show us the suffering and pain constant quarreling inflicts. If we are quarrelsome, we might learn to change by recognizing why we are that way. The proverbs indicates that some people are contentious because they are impulsive. Not realizing the damage they cause, they spontaneously turn every issue into an argument. "Every fool is quick to quarrel" (20:3). Fools are too proud to admit to God that they are wrong. We should not be like this fool who loves to fight, since "he who loves a quarrel loves sin" (17:19).

Remedies for an Ill Humor

Sometimes the quarrelsome person is not deliberately so. Proverbs recognizes the existence of a "bad temper." "A hot-tempered man stirs up dissension, but a patient man calms a quarrel" (15:18). Being short on temper is a major-league struggle for some people. Their tempers are inside them like caged monsters, and they're never sure when they'll have that uncontrollable impulse to turn the monsters loose. I sensed deep heartache in a middle-aged man who told me what the angry beast in him had done to his family life. His wife had defended herself from his outbursts by becoming indifferent and distant. His daughter hated him. "What can I do about it? I've been a Christian for decades, but I've never been able to control my outbursts," he said. I've heard this same plea enough to know that short tempers are not in short supply—even among Christians. Recently, leaders of a church denomination asked their pastors what kind of training their church families needed the most. Topping the list was "dealing with conflict." When ministers' wives were asked what they and their husbands most needed help with, over sixty percent put dealing with anger in the home first.

Sometimes the anger is kept inside, solidified into a seething resentment. At times, the frozen anger thaws and spills over like boiling water, scalding those it touches.

That getting a grip on anger is a major human problem should not surprise us. While anger itself is not wrong as a human emotion, it is a major human problem. Note how many of the sins in the Apostle Paul's list have to do with anger: "The acts of the sinful nature are obvious: sexual immorality, impurity and debauchery; idolatry and witchcraft; hatred, discord, jealousy, fits of rage, selfish ambition, dissensions, factions and envy; drunkenness, orgies, and the like" (Gal. 5:19-21). To emphasize this problem Paul piles up words for anger in his letter to the Ephesians: "Get rid of all bitterness, rage and anger, brawling and slander, along with every form of malice" (Eph. 4:31). Rage has been a family problem ever since it led Cain to slaughter his brother, Abel. The answer to anger lies in the power of God's Spirit. The fruit of the Spirit should counteract it. Love, joy, peace, longsuffering, patience: these are the opposites of anger and the cures for it.

That the ultimate answer is spiritual, however, need not keep us from trying to deal with the personal causes of a bad or short temper. Proverbs has something to say about this. But we must recognize that Proverbs doesn't have all the answers to the problem. Modern science has found evidence linking anger to body chemistry. A condition called hypoglycemia can release into the system huge amounts of adrenaline, the hormone that prepares a person to fight and to face emergencies. With this chemical surging through his or her arteries, a person overreacts to the slightest annoyances. The answer to this condition is controlling the intake of sugar. A verse of Scripture will not help as much as a new diet. The brain's chemistry can also create an angry person. Researchers aren't certain what causes the problem, but they have established a link between the brain's physical condition and a person's emotional state. Before attributing a bad temper to inner corruption or Satanic powers, a trip to a physician is in order. The cure may be as near as his office.

Proverbs offers aid to those whose bad tempers may be a spiritual and emotional problem. Inflexibility could be the major culprit. In Proverbs, in the original language, being quick-tempered is compared to having a short nose or shortness of breath. The wise man of Proverbs 14:29 has a long nose (is patient) while the stupid person is short of breath (quick-tempered), according to the Hebrew. The patient person takes a deep breath as he holds his anger in abeyance. A patient ruler is dubbed "the long of breath" (25:15). The Hebrew word for temper in 14:29 refers to pliability in metal, which must sometimes bend or flex in response to conditions. As pliability is a strength to metal, it is a virtue to persons. An ill-tempered person is one who is too unyielding. By remaining too rigid, he breaks under pressure—like a fool. To lengthen your temper, you must become more flexible. Much of our anger comes from trying to force our wills on others. When others don't go along, righteous indignation boils into plain old wrath.

Persons who are too angry must ask themselves if they are too unbending. They should search their hearts and their pasts to see why. There are many possible causes: disappointment that life hasn't turned out as expected; desire to shore up a sagging self-image; guilt feelings; fear that if you bend a little, you'll lose your convictions and morals.

Marriage experts tell us plainly that healthy families are made up of flexible people. Unhealthy families tend toward rigidity. Members of families without emotional flexibility have poorer psychological health than those that have it (Myron F. Weiner, "Healthy and Pathological Love—Psychodynamic Views," in Kenneth S. Pope et al., *On Love and Loving*, Jossey-Bass Publishers, 1980, p. 127).

Proverbs says that it's not only the quick-tempered that cause strife. "A greedy man stirs up dissension" (28:25). That the love of money causes fights may account for the fact that the number one subject of domestic arguments is finances. The answer to this dissatisfied lust for more and more is found in the rest of the proverb: "but he who trusts in the Lord will prosper." Reliance on God will quench the restless discontent created by our materialism and consumerism. At peace with our desires, we will be more at peace with others.

A foolish view of dissension may underlie some people's tendency to fly off the handle. Deep down inside, they haven't been convinced that when they blow their top, they blow it. They don't control their anger because they condone such behavior. Last week I had lunch with a wise man and his grown son. He had established an economic development committee in his city. When he told of the indifference of local politicians to what they were doing, his son said, "Boy, would I have let them have it." The wise man replied, "I used to think that it was best to spout off whenever I felt like it; but then I read in Proverbs that being coolheaded beats being a hero or a conqueror" (Prov. 16:32). He had learned that angry outbursts aren't the means to progress. James concurs: "Man's anger does not bring about the righteous life that God desires" (James 1:20).

Proper Clash Disposal

Angry outbursts cause marital discord. Researcher Maggie Hayes urges couples in mid-life to especially be aware of the role of anger in their relationships. Nagging, sarcasm, criticism are all warning signs of corrosion in the marriage. We need constructive ways of handling anger and discord.

Ignore some of the garbage. First, learn to ignore trespasses against you. "It is to [a person's] glory to overlook offenses" (19:11). We resist this. We want to fight; we want to make an issue of things. Maybe it's because of our pride, or perhaps we're afraid to let someone get away with something. Whatever the reason, the wise person knows that forgiving and forgetting are part of the price of peace and love. It was such a wise woman who said, "My husband won't pick up his socks, but he's such a wonderful husband otherwise, who cares?" It's a wise man who says, "My wife doesn't clean house as I would like; at times it's honorable to look the other way."

IMPROVING YOUR CLASH ASSETS

Don't use an incinerator. Proverbs warns us about the amount of heat we allow into our discussions. Once you start quarreling, it's like digging a hole in a dam. A trickle quickly becomes a torrent. "So drop the matter before a dispute breaks out" (17:14). Don't let the intensity build. You may end up in court (the Hebrew word for "dispute" sometimes is a judicial term). Essentially Jesus said the same thing: "As you are going with your adversary to the magistrate, try hard to be reconciled to him on the way, or he may drag you off to the judge, and the judge turn you over to the officer, and the officer throw you into prison" (Luke 12:58) (from Alden, *Proverbs,* Baker Books, p. 135). In marriage we continually have to weigh the issue against the hassle. A psychiatrist who is a professor at the University of Texas says precisely that. "Healthy people who love each other are able to resolve difficulties by compromises that avoid name-calling and that enhance the partner's sense of potency" (Myron F. Weiner, "Healthy and Pathological Love," in Pope, p. 127).

Avoid calling your partner's arguments "rubbish." Watch what you say, another proverb advises: "A gentle answer turns away wrath, but a harsh word stirs up anger" (15:1). Too often we counter anger instead of cool it. It's so easy to blame our partner for being angry or to counterattack by pointing out that they're just as bad as you are. It's tough to be gentle or even quiet. James says we can defend ourselves from anger by "being slow to speak" (James 1:19). But speech control is not easy. The old remedies are still effective: walking around the block, chopping wood, chomping on your tongue. James gives another suggestion: "Be quick to listen" (James 1:19). It's sometimes smart to be dumb. Careful listening is an antidote to rash speaking. Too often we play the fool: "He who answers before listening—that is his folly and his shame" (Prov. 18:13). That comes from a quirk in many a character: "A fool finds no pleasure in understanding but delights in airing his own opinions" (18:2). One researcher said that his experiment showed that 85% of messages in our homes were misunderstood. If true, that explains why talking so often converts to scrapping. Overtones of ill feeling make us churlish, bearish, and snappish. Harsh, scornful, and insensitive words pollute our families like odorous vapors. As I grow older, I pray more, "God, enable my lips to be the source of the word aptly spoken—that my words be like apples of gold in settings of silver" (Prov. 25:11). Carelessly offending one another closes us up to one another and strains our love. "An offended brother is more unyielding than a fortified city, and disputes are like the barred gates of a citadel" (18:19).

Let someone else wrap it up. One more proverb adds to our guidelines for dealing with conflict. "Casting the lot settles disputes and keeps strong opponents apart" (18:18). Casting a lot, like tossing a coin, was used in ancient times to settle issues. This proverb speaks of disputes between mighty foes, who, if the lot did not give them a means of settlement, would meet their demands by violence (Franz Delitzsch, *Biblical Commentary on the Proverbs of Solomon*, Wm. B. Eerdmans Publishing Co., vol. II, p. 12). Unlike our tossing a coin, however, there was a spiritual significance to deciding by lot among the Hebrews. "The lot is cast into the lap, but its every decision is from the Lord" (16:33). This verse tells of how God is in control of human affairs. It may not mean that we should make decisions or solve disputes by a toss of the coin. (But why not, if after discussion, a husband and wife aren't agreed?) What Proverbs does teach is that an outside third party can help us with our disputes. While that third party may be a cast lot, a judge, or a counselor, it should mostly be the Lord. Couples will agree most when they both agree with God. The closer we conform to God's will, the closer we'll be to one another. God's Word offers us the wisdom and insight to know what is right and just and fair (Prov. 1:3). The pursuit of personal wisdom is also the pursuit of interpersonal peace.

Chapter
TEN

THE MA AND PA INSTITUTE OF HIGHER LEARNING

>Father's instruction... mother's teaching.
>PROVERBS 1:8

Columnist Ann Landers asked parents whether or not, given the choice again, they would choose to have children. Over 60% said, "No way." Other surveys indicate the Landers' survey results were way off and that less than 20% wish they never had children. Still, there are a lot of unhappy parents. Catherine Brown put it bluntly: "As all parents and non-parents know, life with children can be hell" ("It Changed My Life," *Psychology Today,* November 1976, p. 47). It is generally true that a couple's marital satisfaction hits its lowest point when couples have teens and goes back to a high level when the children leave home.

Modern Parent Syndrome
Parents are confused and uncertain. One expert put it this way: "Whatever grandfather did was done with authority; whatever we do is done with hesitation. Even when in error, grandfather acted with certainty. Even when in the right, we act with doubt" (Haim Ginott, *Between Parent and Child,* Macmillan, 1965, p. 91).

Parents are filled with guilt. Teachers put the finger on them if their kids won't learn; the community accuses them if the kids have troubles; and the youth director scolds them because their teens hate to attend youth meetings. As one expert says, "Today parents are blamed, not trained."

Everyone will agree that parenting is as challenging a task as a person can undertake. I had lunch with a prominent surgeon last week, and he confided that being a parent is much harder than being a doctor. When 10,467 parents in an adolescence-parent study were asked about parenting, four out of five agreed that "to be a good parent is one of the hardest things in life I do" (Merton P. Strommen and A. Irene Strommen, *Five Cries of Parents,* Harper & Row, p. 12). There are corporate executives who drive around the block several times to get the courage to go home and face the family, aware that it's easier to command a large staff of people across a desk than to communicate with a teenage son across the dining room table.

The Ragged Edges of the Extreme
The difficult task of parenting demands a proper attitude at the start. Proverbs helps us avoid two extreme views of parenting. First, there is the "neglectful parent." For whatever reason, this parent isn't there when the child needs him or her. This person usually dislikes or devalues being a parent. The results are sorrowful: "A child left to itself disgraces his mother" (29:15). In need of thousands of kisses, hugs, rebukes, compliments, and countless other things, children are not self-sufficient. A famous study strikingly showed how badly kids need parents. In a South American orphanage a doctor observed the plight of ninety-seven babies, three months to three years of age. Because a shortage of funds reduced the staff to a pitiful few, these children received nothing but basic care. Mouths were fed, diapers changed, and once in a while bodies washed. Between feedings and changes, there was no cuddling to a mother's breast, no soft words of love, melodious songs, nor a father's playful antics.

Even though they had physical care, in three months

symptoms of abnormality appeared. Many lost their appetites and were unable to sleep. Faces had a vacant expression. In five months, major deterioration had set in. They lay whimpering, trembling, faces twisted in pain. Some screamed in terror when picked up by a staff member. Twenty-seven children died the first year, seven more the next. Only twenty-one of the ninety-seven survived, these with serious emotional damage. Parents are most conspicuous by their absence. The role of a parent is no option. Those who slight it will see the ugly fruit of neglect.

A person can swing to the other extreme, that of trying to be an "omnipotent parent." Parents in this frame of mind are driven by an overblown view of a parent's power. A child is a piece of putty they mold or fail to mold into the right image (usually theirs). They improperly interpret Proverbs 22:6 to mean that what they impart, the child will not depart from. One of these parents shook my hand at the rear of the church where I had just spoken, sharing her pride that all of her children were Christians. "How do you account for that?" I asked. "I just decided that they'd be Christians or I'd kill 'em," burst from her lips, eyes flashing a mixture of humor and determination. A strong sense of responsibility combines with a wrong idea about parenting to create this type of parent. In their minds children are machines given to us by God. The Bible tells us precisely what buttons to push and levers to pull to create the desired effect. If the machine doesn't produce, the operator is at fault.

This unrealistic view of a parent's potency can generate a lot of anxiety. One mistake and the child is doomed to a wasted life and perhaps even hell. Discipline and decisions are made out of fear. Instead of experiencing love and acceptance, a child suffers under pressure and perfectionism. Any symptom of trouble in the child sets the parent reeling with remorse, looking back to see where they went wrong. "We shouldn't have allowed him to buy that first rock record," or "We didn't spank her enough," or maybe, "We spanked her too much."

So convinced that they are the shapers of Johnny, "superparents" can't imagine being at peace with themselves if their children don't turn out right. Sometimes Christian leaders foster this attitude in their attempts to motivate people to be good parents. "What have you got left if you're children don't turn out right?" I heard Tim LaHaye say on TV. Concerned for American family life, this dedicated man was warning young parents to be serious about parenting. In the process, however, he exaggerated the parental task. I wanted to be able to say to the viewers, "There's something left: your life." Too often, I have watched parents permit a troubled teenager not only to ruin his own life but pull the house down on everyone else. Proverbs reminds us that sometimes the child is at fault, and parents are not omnipotent. It's not always that fathers don't discipline; sometimes "a fool spurns his father's discipline" (15:5). Not only do parents fail their children; children can fail their parents: "a foolish son" brings grief to his mother (10:1). Not only do fathers ruin children; "a foolish son is his father's ruin" (19:13). Face it, there are children who defy the wisest experts' attempts to understand them.

Children are not machines, like computers, with parents the all-powerful programmers. Children have their own programs and many other people play a role in programming them. The child is not the product of the parents. Parents have no right being proud if their child follows Christ, nor need they unnecessarily blame themselves if he or she doesn't. To avoid the extremes, we need to recognize that we have an important role to play, but not an all-powerful one. Trusting God, we do our best.

Sparing the Word Worse Than Sparing the Rod

What demands our best, according to Proverbs, is the task of teaching. Just as Proverbs asserts that having wisdom is essential to godly living, it asserts that sharing wisdom is central to good parenting. At first this may sound strange, since Proverbs is more popularly known for what it says about spanking. But the teaching of the Word is more important than the wielding of the paddle. Sparing the Word is far worse than sparing the rod.

Parents are the major bestowers of wisdom, according to the book of Proverbs. Giving credit to his father, the wise man says, "When I was a boy in my father's house . . . he taught me" (4:3-4). Children are repeatedly told to follow the teaching of both father and mother: "Listen, my son, to your father's instruction and do not forsake your mother's teaching" (1:8; see also 4:1; 6:20; 23:22).

Listening to a father's teaching is more than hearing what he has to say. Forsaking a mother's teaching is not just forgetting it. In the Hebrew mind, hearing and not forsaking parental teaching meant obeying it.

Imparting wisdom requires more than getting a child to memorize Bible verses. Wisdom includes respect for God and His truth and a desire to follow it. That requires helping a child see the good results of living by wisdom and the bad effects of not living by wisdom. This is the essence of child training or instruction, *musar* in Hebrew. Most often, this discipline (*musar*) is done through oral instruction. In other words, the parent tells how blessing will follow such and such a behavior. Discipline (*musar*) can also take the form of a warning: don't do this, or such and such will happen. Given the nature of discipline (*musar*), it can also be taught through the rod of correction: "The rod of correction imparts wisdom" (29:15). God Himself uses life's wounds and pains to chastise us. In His school of hard knocks we learn that we reap what we sow. God is not asking for blind obedience, but wise compliance. Parents have the same objective. Spanking a child is not like giving a shock to a white rat, conditioning it to turn left instead of right. Disciplining a child must result in more than his making a right turn; it must result in his knowing why he turned right. That is wisdom. Teaching must be in consort with corporal punishment. Because it is the more important part of discipline, we will begin with teaching.

Incite to Insight
Unlike some systems of education, the Bible portrays children as being badly in need of knowledge. Ideas are not inside of them, like undeveloped photographs, that slowly appear like Polaroid prints when children are stimulated to think for themselves. Nor do they merely get ideas from experience, as if the only way for them to learn is to knock their heads against life's concrete. The Book of Proverbs plainly states that the child needs to be taught. Proverbs was written "for giving prudence to the simple" (1:4). Children are described as innocent and flexible, inclined to believe anything they hear (14:15); they need wise teachers (1:5). Teaching will not be easy, since children will sometimes resist learning (7:7). But workable guidelines emerge from the Proverbs.

Teach the child to love wisdom. Love of wisdom is the mark of the mature person (29:3). Fools despise wisdom (1:7). They quarrel against "sound wisdom" and want to follow their own desires (18:1). Building respect for wisdom is one of the major goals of child rearing. Proverbs places a high price tag on wisdom. Mom's and Dad's instruction is compared to "a graceful wreath" for the head and "ornaments" for around the neck (1:9, NASB). It's better to get wisdom than gold—understanding than silver (8:10). In other words, wisdom is elegant and priceless because it ensures personal peace, satisfaction, and fulfillment. Without it, life would be a catastrophe.

To instill this respect for wisdom, Proverbs reminds us of its consequences. God's truth always has this moral character to it. Knowledge shapes behavior, which produces a quality life. Wisdom will yield one thing, folly another.

To help our children, we parents must cultivate our own respect for wisdom. To develop inches of respect in them, we will need yards of it ourselves. Then there's a good chance our attitude will be "caught" by them.

We can also develop respect by reminding them of the consequences of their actions. We'll have to be careful here, since children don't like to be preached at all the time. We don't have to sprinkle a warning into every conversation. We need to be wise about *how* we teach as well as *what* we teach. This guideline also comes from Proverbs.

Make your teaching palatable. Parents don't discharge their responsibility by merely handing down morals without considering how they do it. Some people constantly quarrel with their children, brutally point out their faults, offer little affirmation, and angrily dictate rules with little explanation or compassion. The advice they give may be right, but their method of giving it wrong. The wise share wisdom wisely. "A wise man's heart guides his mouth" (16:23). Persuasion requires "pleasant words" (16:21). The wise make words as pleasant as honey, which is sweet to the soul, bringing healing to the bones (16:24). Doing this may not require genius, but it will demand some creativity. Proverbs are amazingly creative—perhaps as an example to us.

The Formal Approach

Create some special teaching moments. Teaching formally doesn't demand turning our living rooms into classrooms. Home life has an informal quality that we can capitalize on. Nor does the emphasis on homemade Christian education mean we can do without our church programs. Biblical teaching should take place at both home and church. There are effective formal ways to teach: reading books, listening to records, having family devotional times. There are many fine resources to use with your children. The stories, lessons, and songs in these materials are as palatable as sugar-coated grain. I've seen children wear out these books and records while digesting life-changing ideas.

Family devotion times are a good teaching opportunity. The Bible doesn't really command this practice. It tells us to teach our children, but doesn't insist we have daily devotions. If not carefully done, family devotions can have a negative impact. Many young people have been turned off and "case-hardened" by this daily routine. This is partly true because it's tough to keep this day-after-day ritual from being boring. I have had seminary students who said they became Christians "in spite of," not "because of," family devotions. But other Christian people confirm that, if done well, family devotions can be effective. Since there is little research to help us in this area, I offer the following guidelines, which I have gleaned from various sources.

Do what's personally best for you and your family. What fits your family is no doubt best for your family. One dedicated Christian father told a group of pastors in my seminar about his family's devotional practice. For the past twenty years his large family has read the Bible, prayed, and sang hymns together every morning, at times as early as 6:30 A.M. His children had eventually memorized a whole hymnbook. Three of them are in full-time ministry.

There is a strong temptation to copy that man and his wife. But for various reasons, not all Christian parents could do as they have done. Better we do what is suited for our family instead of imitating what may be too difficult for us to maintain.

Make family devotions regular. Determine the best time and place and try to stick with it. What doesn't get into our schedule usually doesn't get into our lives. Scheduling doesn't guarantee we always have our daily devotions. Sometimes the pace is hectic, and adjustments have to be made. This doesn't render our planning worthless. Better to aim for something and hit it once in a while than to aim for nothing at all. Nor does it seem necessary to have devotions every day. Some families skip it on Sunday when they are worshiping together at church and on Wednesday, when the family members may be in small groups or club meetings.

Keep devotions simple. It may be possible to make family devotions too complicated and creative. The everyday demand of coming up with something may make it hard to maintain them. Better to do something that's easily done: read from a good book; read a Bible passage and ask the children a few questions; or do some informal sharing and praying.

Make devotions short. Being brief may be the best way to keep devotions from the city limits of Dullsville. This doesn't mean every session will be a brief one. If kids start asking questions, the time might be extended. Once in a while our devotions went on for an hour, but it was spontaneous and unplanned.

Plan ahead. Keeping devotions simple doesn't rule out planning. Someone has to determine what book of the Bible will be read next, what translation will be used, or if a Bible storybook will be read. With a little planning, you can produce some variety for each evening, like having a missionary story on Tuesdays or a special time of sharing on Thursday.

Allow for participation. Though this sounds simple, this principle is not easily applied. When seven-year-old Kevin reads the passage of Scripture for the family, this may be just the thing to hold his interest. But his stumbling along may not keep his fourteen-year-old brother, Larry, on the edge of his seat. Because the age span was so large between our children, Ginger and I once split our kids into two groups in order to involve them. Their participation is a key to their enthusiasm for devotions.

Permit spontaneity and make devotions relational. Our relating to God can also occasion our relating to one another. Devotion time can provoke some in-depth sharing with one another. Try asking questions about feeling: "How does this passage make you feel?" "Were you ever depressed like the psalmist in the passage?" "What makes you depressed?" "What brings you out of depression?" Or encourage personal sharing about needs and attitudes. "What fruit of the Spirit do you most need?" "What are you thankful for?" We can get to know each other better and in the process affirm and help one another.

The Walk-Talk Approach

Capitalize on informal opportunities to teach. Interestingly, in the Bible the cornerstone of child training is not formal teaching. In chapter six of Deuteronomy, the most important passage about teaching children, the stress falls on the informal. The phrase, "you shall teach them diligently" is a translation of a Hebrew word that normally means "to sharpen" (Deut. 6:7, NASB). Apparently Moses was using it as a metaphor to indicate that teaching should be like sharpening a sword—it takes a lot of stroking back and forth, a constant repetition. "Impress them on your children," another translation says (NIV). And the way to do this is contained in the next phrase: "Talk about them when you sit at home and when you walk along the road, when you lie down and when you get up" (Deut. 6:7). Perhaps the home is best suited for this informal instruction. Formal teaching runs the danger of being too intellectual and unrelated to life. A child is saturated with words about Christianity without having an opportunity to experience them. An informal situation is less likely to be so bookish and academic.

Taking that as a cue, let's explore some avenues that will open up talking about God around the house. For starters, most of us need to discover more ways to get us talking —about anything. Part of the problem we have in bringing God into our conversations is that there is so little conversation to begin with. In-depth talk doesn't flow easily from contemporary home life. One sociologist says that one appliance has destroyed conversation in our homes more than any other—the automatic dishwasher. He's kidding, of course, but he makes a good point. Working together, like washing dishes, prompts conversation. Having more family activities will foster more small talk, which can lead to significant discussions.

My wife has had her most meaningful conversations with our children in the kitchen, when they were working together. When my grown sons visit our home, they still converse in the kitchen, dangling their legs from the kitchen counter. One woman shares how walking has built ties with family members. She took note of how going for a walk with one of her children stimulated them to talk. This led her to do the same with her other children. Eventually, she invited her husband. Now, the whole family walks together—and talks.

Not only should we deliberately work at making conversation, we will also need to give some thought to how to insert Scripture into our discussions. It must not be so artificial and unnatural that it seems out of place and insincere. I'm not sure modern kids can handle a parent who is always popping off with *King James* verses in an unnatural way. I got a picture of this once when I was staying in someone's home. Walking into the kitchen in the morning, I heard, "Good morning, Dr. Sell, this is a day the Lord hath made and we shall rejoice and be glad in it." I was a bit stunned. Everyone else says something like, "Hi, Dr. Sell—did you sleep well?" Though I respected the elderly woman who had greeted me, I wondered how her kids might have felt if they got Bible verses flung at them like that. It's important that God's Word comes across as genuine and relevant.

To do this, we might make Scripture part of an affirmation. "You were kind to her, Eddie; that's important since the Bible says, 'Be kind to one another.'" Or, include Scripture in an answer to a problem: "I struggle with worrying, too; I find that praying helps since Scripture tells us to pray and not be anxious about things that bother us."

Proverbs indicates that it is OK to rebuke a child. "The rod of correction imparts wisdom," according to Proverbs 29:15. Most parents are careful about including God and Scripture in their rebukes since they don't want to turn God into a heavenly policeman.

Happy, inspirational times are opportunities to refer to our Lord: when looking at a sunset, viewing a rainbow, or hiking through a scenic forest. Natural surroundings almost always seem to make us think of God.

Even when Scripture is not quoted, God's truth can be

taught, particularly when we seek to find analogies from life. This can be one of the most effective ways, since life itself has a lot of examples of Christian ideas. A friend told me of his experience with his son last summer. His boy had found a new bicycle submerged in a small creek behind his house. They took it to the police, where they learned it would belong to the finder if no one claimed it in three months' time. No one did. When picking it up, they were told of another regulation: the boy could use the bicycle, but if anyone made a legitimate claim within the next year, he would have to give it up. My friend used this unique experience to say to his son, "You have a great chance to learn one of life's great lessons. All of our possessions are like this bicycle. They are on loan to us and can be taken away at any time. We must enjoy them and be grateful as long as they are ours to use." No doubt that lesson was driven home repeatedly whenever the boy grew anxious about losing his bike.

Another way to insert God's Word into our talk is to take advantage of questions. Answering questions is a golden opportunity to teach. That's what makes home an even more opportune place than school. Real living prompts real questions at home. Children often ask thousands of questions each year. Parents can watch for them and share God's truth from memory or else run for their Bibles, concordances, or Bible dictionaries.

Children often ask questions casually because it reduces the threat of asking them. When troubled, yet afraid to ask for help, they may subtly work their question into a conversation. One of my sons was thinking through a sensitive matter. It popped up while we were shooting baskets in the driveway. "Dad, how do we know that the Bible is true? (*swoosh*) I mean, wasn't it written by ordinary people a long time ago?" (*swoosh*) "Well son, that's a good question. I'm glad you're thinking about—oops, missed—such important issues." I went on to discuss the kinds of things we talk about in a seminary classroom—right there in the driveway. I knew from what he said a few days later that he had jumped a major hurdle in his life—for the time being he would trust the Bible and keep working on the issue of its truthfulness and authority.

A Christian leader told me this story: A man had begun teaching the Bible to his young daughter. She told her friend about it. To her own father, the friend said, "Daddy, will you teach me the Bible like Emily's father is doing?"

That little girl's plea hits hard. Meeting our children's spiritual and moral needs is a deeply felt issue with today's Christian parents. Contemporary life doesn't make that job easy. While writing this chapter, I said to myself repeatedly, "I wish I had done better as my children's teacher." Along with a lot of other parents, I console myself with the thought that I tried—very hard.

Any inheritance of faith we leave will be the best inheritance. Perhaps our children will eventually do what the wise man urges: "Keep your father's commands and do not forsake your mother's teaching. Bind them upon your heart forever; fasten them around your neck" (6:20-21). If they do, they will have received a very special legacy. When they walk about, that teaching will guide them; when they sleep, it will watch over them; and when they are awake, it will talk to them (6:22).

Chapter
ELEVEN

DESIGNER DISCIPLINE

Discipline... in that there is hope.
PROVERBS 19:18

A few months ago, an accident on our block sent tremors of fear through the neighborhood. An eight-year-old girl lay on the street outside her home, her smashed bicycle lying beside her, the driver of the car that hit her near panic. Nervous and excited children formed a circle around her, while parents comforted her and waited for an ambulance. Though her injuries turned out to be minor, the impact of the accident was major. For weeks parents noted how no children were carelessly darting from their driveways onto the street as they had been the day of the accident.

Like all of us, children learn from the experiences of others. Certain proverbs confirm this. "Flog a mocker, and the simple will learn prudence" (19:25). The public punishment of the scoffer gives wisdom to the naive who see it.

An Eventful Way to Shape Values

Providing experiences for our children is a powerful means of teaching them. Experiences do more than shape what they know; they change what they value. Parents can do this kind of "valuing" with their children by putting together the answers to two questions: What characteristics do my children need? What experiences will help shape those characteristics? They need things like respect for others, ability to give affection, self-respect, a sense of well-being, Christian morals and ethics, and a sense of responsibility. Drawing upon a passage like 1 Peter 1:5-7, we can make a fine list of such Christian virtues: faith (trust in God), goodness (respect for virtue), knowledge (desire to have wisdom and truth), self-control (self-discipline and respect for authority), perseverance (ability to endure and finish a job), godliness (being serious about God), brotherly kindness (respect and affection for others), and love (willingness to sacrifice for others).

Aware of these, think of the types of experiences that will build these into a child's life. If we list some categories of life's experiences, we can see a variety of alternatives.

- Being exposed to examples (such as a camp counselor during the summer).
- Relating to others in depth (such as sharing prayer requests in a youth group).
- Reading (such as missionary biographies).
- Doing activities that are related to nature and animals (such as caring for a pet).
- Participating in large-group activities (such as spectator sports).
- Participating in small-group activities (such as a planning committee for a social).
- Being a leader (such as being a junior club leader).
- Serving (such as doing service projects at church).
- Making decisions (such as participating in family decisions about vacations).
- Participating in discussions (such as dinnertime conversation).
- Having responsibilities (such as a family chore: taking out the garbage cans regularly).
- Doing things that develop skills (such as archery lessons).

- Taking part in hobbies, sports, music, recreation (such as playing in the school band).
- Being in educational experiences (school, of course, but also special classes in the summer time or at church).

Valuing requires matching the child's experience to some virtue that needs to take shape in his character. Let's suppose you want to develop *responsibility*. These are the types of experiences you might want your child to have: completing assigned chores at home, participating in family discussions and decisions, participating in camp and other activities that bring the child into contact with responsible people, reading biographies and stories that show the value of acting responsibly, and choosing a pet to care for.

The above list is only suggestive. Responsibility can be developed in countless ways. Children don't have to excel in everything they do to gain a sense of personal responsibility and self-discipline. One of my sons, for example, was quite average in most things he undertook. We were unable to push him to continue trumpet lessons beyond a few years; he got by at school but was not highly motivated. The only thing he really excelled in was hunting and fishing. My wife and I weren't ecstatic over his putting endless hours into reading *Field and Stream* and his rising early mornings to head for a lake or woods. Concerned, we talked to an acquaintance, the president of a Christian college. "You'll be surprised," he said, "by the discipline, character, and skills your boy is developing through his dedication to outdoor activities." He told of his own grown son who at one time had devoted himself to a hobby, while being quite average in other areas of life. The hobby experience had prepared the way for his college success as well as his excelling in his vocation. We took heart; the same became true for our boy. Hunting and fishing contributed to turning him into a responsible and successful adult and an above-average learner.

A Model Approach

Since experience is such a powerful teacher, children will also learn from their experience of us. Research confirms that their lives are shaped by what we model for them. Consider this study: nursery-school children observed a film depicting an adult punching, hitting, and kicking a big, inflated plastic clown. Some children saw the adult get rewarded for abusing the toy clown—he was given some candy for what he had done. Other children saw a person punished for what he did to the clown—he was scolded by another adult. A third group of children saw nothing happen to the adult who beat up the clown.

After viewing the films, children were left alone with the clown doll. Those who had seen the person on the film punished tended to avoid hitting the clown, as compared to those in the other two groups of children. These researchers proved scientifically what the proverb says: if a scoffer gets punished for his behavior, children will learn not to scoff (A. Bandura, P. Ross, and A. Ross, "Vicarious Reinforcement and Imitative Learning," quoted in *Educational Psychology: A Contemporary View,* pp. 65-66).

Children will learn a great deal from watching us. Proverbs 10:17 states it clearly: "He who heeds discipline shows the way to life, but whoever ignores correction leads others astray." By growing in Christ, parents help their children grow. Whether our modeling is positive or negative, it will affect our children. One of the hardest parts for me of having teens was seeing how they had copied so many of my bad traits. They follow our examples even when we don't want them to. Once when I was trying to do what a person does in a study, I was interrupted by my young son's shouting. From the second floor of the house, he was yelling for his mother, who was out in the yard. Though my study was in the basement, his shouts reached me, but not her. When he didn't stop, I finally bellowed, "Howie, don't yell in the house." I had betrayed my words without even realizing it. Modeling is tough work. But the hard effort we put into our own maturity will be an investment in our children's. If we are growing, they will be growing too.

Our modeling will have to be genuine to be effective. If we're not careful, our attempts to be good examples can turn us into hypocrites. Modeling is not acting like a Christian for the kid's sakes when they're around to see us. Our faith must be real. If not, kids will see through our little act. They know us too well to be fooled.

If you pretend to be up when you're down or glad when sad, your modeling is insincere. Kids don't like hypocrites any more than we adults do. One thirteen-year-old boy was talking to me about his dad. "He's easy to talk to," he said. "I like him. One day he was teaching us from the Book of Acts in our Sunday School class. Ananias and Sapphira were liars: God didn't like that. My dad said, 'I don't want to be a phony.' That really changed my mind about him—I thought all adults were phonies. But not my dad. Now that I know that, we have a good relationship."

By being unreal, we not only lose our kids' respect, we also lose a good chance to teach them. Kids need examples of how to handle the so-called negative things of life. We need to show them our depression so they can accept and deal with theirs. We ought to be open about our conflicts with others so they can see how to manage it themselves. One Christian father told me his grown children said to him, "Dad, you taught us how to succeed, but you didn't teach us how to fail." Letting them in on our faults and failures can teach them how to cope with life.

Something else should be emphasized about modeling: kids follow the example of the persons they're close to. Modeling involves identifying with someone, not just imitating them. Imitating merely means doing something we see someone else do, like watching an adult to find out how to get candy out of a machine. Modeling happens whenever there is a strong emotional bond between the model and the follower. Research proves that a child strives to be like the person he loves. If we want our child to be like us, he or she must like us. The Book of Proverbs develops respect for the wise by continually exalting them. We can develop respect in our children through closeness—by being open with them. Not that our children should follow everything we do; they need to develop their own personalities, tastes, and interests. But our influence will be powerful if they identify spiritually and morally with us. The greatest compliment ever given to me was inscribed on a Father's Day card. "Dad, I want to be like you," my teenager wrote. Not all my children have said that. But my wife, Ginger, and I have learned that being intimate with our children is a big part of being influential.

What we have said about modeling is good news. We can change our children by changing ourselves. Changing someone else is tough. Changing myself is difficult—but possible. God promises me power for that. I can work on my children's maturity by working on mine.

The bad news is this: modeling is not enough. Good models don't always produce model children. That's simply because we are not our children's only models. There are many models around—and many of them bad. Being an exemplary Christian doesn't guarantee your children will be Christians.

Our own modeling needs to be supplemented by that of others. "He who walks with the wise men grows wise" (Proverbs 13:20). There are many ways Christian parents can get their children to keep company with mature Christians. Programs offered by the church, like clubs, camping, and Sunday School can do this. Intergenerational activities that include adults, youth, and children worshiping, sharing, praying, playing, and studying together can expose our children to good examples. In our church we have times when all ages share problems and needs and then pray for each other. In addition we have creative intergenerational events. Also, in small groups in the homes, whole families fellowship together. The results in my own children have been profound. When my son filled out a camp application, he was asked about how youth sponsors had influenced him. He wrote, "Not only have youth leaders contributed to me spiritually, but many adults in my church have."

The Negative Means to Positive Results

Sometimes training a child includes correction, both verbal and physical. "The rod of correction imparts wisdom" (Prov. 29:15). Wisdom comes from a stick the same way it comes from our teaching and our modeling; it shows that wrong acts produce negative results. Warn a child not to cross a highway, and he may be old enough and wise enough to heed. But when a toddler is headed for a busy street, there is no time to talk. When after repeated rebukes a child disobeys, it may be time for action.

Correction should be done, according to Proverbs, but it should be done right. One of the right ways to do it is be sure that it teaches instead of punishes. Good discipline looks to the future, aiming to teach a lesson, not to get even. All forms of discipline are for the child's education, just like God's discipline of us. "God disciplines us for our good, that we may share in His holiness" (Heb. 12:10). Good discipline is measured by how much a child learns, not by how much it hurts. Parents will have peace of mind and delight from a well-disciplined child (Prov. 29:17). But that doesn't mean they should discipline to keep the child from bothering them. (*Whack!* "Move, don't get in front of the TV screen.") Rather, their joy comes from having a wise child.

Disciplining is loving. "He who spares the rod hates his son, but he who loves him is careful to discipline him" (13:24). For this reason, both the parents' discipline and God's discipline should be welcomed "because the Lord disciplines those He loves, as a father the son he delights in" (3:12). Warnings of discipline from God are not threats, they're promises. We can count on God to be a faithful Father and not let us get out of line to our own destruction. Parents, like God, show love by being faithful disciplinarians, since the benefits to the child are so great. Not only will it drive out foolishness (Prov. 22:15), it will purge the inmost being (20:30) and perhaps save the child from an untimely death. "If you punish him with the rod, he will not die. Punish him with the rod and save his soul from death" (23:13-14). The child may not always see love in your discipline. "I'm doing this because I love you," a father said to his son as he began his spanking. "Sure, Dad," the boy joked. "I'm sorry I'm not big enough to return your love." When children are loved, however, they will usually be wise enough to accept a parent's discipline.

A parent must know when to use negative forms of discipline. A child should not be rebuked or spanked merely because he or she is a child. Sometimes the child is wise enough to listen to teaching. At other times, a corrective reproof is enough. Proverbs suggests that the rod is called for only in moral or dangerous situations. Spanking is for the child, yes, but only when he is acting like the worst of fools, not when he is simply being naive (10:13; 19:29; 26:3). Severe discipline is for those who sin (15:10).

Corporal discipline should be for moral wrongs, not mistakes. A child should not be punished for acts that flow from his immaturity, like knocking over a glass of milk or coming home late because he genuinely forgot the time, something even thirteen-year-olds can do. Parents should discipline especially when the child defies them. Children's tendency to rebel is part of human foolishness. This resistance to authority can spring up very early. When a toddler flagrantly refuses to obey, hits the parent, shouts, or shows other signs of mutiny, a parent must come out on top of the situation.

Not that discipline permits a parent to violently lash out in anger. Spanking should be the most cautious thing a parent does. It was because of child abuse that the Swedes passed a law against spanking. In their eyes, spanking too often leads to abuse, which is a valid point. If a parent is the type of person who typically uses force to solve problems, that parent can sometimes cause more harm than good by spanking. We must teach our children to use force correctly by using it wisely ourselves.

Consider these guidelines. (1) Spank only when you are in control of yourself. Count to ten or always use the same paddle, which forces you to think while you are going to get it. (2) Spank with a stick or an object that will not do harm, not with your hand. Many children are hurt when a parent, used to hitting with his hand, strikes them impulsively in the head or face. (3) Spank only after an explanation. (4) Spank in private. (5) Spank carefully; while it should hurt, it must not injure. If your child is a loved child and consistently getting wiser, a few swats will suffice. "A rebuke impresses a man of discernment more than a hundred lashes a fool" (17:10).

Spanking may be the last measure to resort to, since there are other effective ways of correcting. Wise parents will know how to permit natural consequences to shape a child. Since God also promises to correct, He will be teaching them through experience. Parents can help the child learn by responding properly to these events.

My young son had such an experience. Delighting in the magic light bulb he had just purchased, he took it out of the container as he walked through the door of the shopping mall. I was about to suggest that it would be best to leave it safely in the bag when he dropped it. Midst the shattered glass, I stood wondering how I could best permit him to learn from this. We can sometimes cancel the learning rather than foster it. Yelling angrily, "I told you not to be so careless," creates guilt and directs the child's attention to our anger instead of the lesson of the broken bulb. Showing too much pity can be just as bad. Promising to buy him another one destroys the impact of the lesson. Being overprotective, many parents deprive children of what circumstances might teach them. I decided to do nothing but encourage him in whatever he would decide. "Do you think they'll give me another one if I take the broken one back?" he asked. Since he had paid for it, I didn't interfere, saying, "You can go back and ask them." I was as anxious as he when he approached the counter, because if he had to bear the loss, I would have had to refrain from buying him another one. I was relieved to hear, "Our policy is that as long as you are in the store, you can get a replacement. Had you been out the door, you would have been responsible."

Of course, training children would be easy if negative consequences always immediately followed wrong actions, but life isn't like that. A child can dash across a street or steal something without suffering. Then the parent has to make up some negative consequences, like spanking or isolating the child in his room or denying some privilege. Generally, the punishment should be as directly related to the misbehavior as possible—and fair. For example, if a teen skips school for a drive with his friends, grounding might be appropriate. In modern society, spanking is an embarrassment to a teen. Depriving the youth of evenings with his friends is a way of saying that study comes before fun. This is just and consistent with life.

Don Dinkmeyer and Gary McKay, the authors of *Systematic Training for Effective Parenting* (American Guidance Service, Inc., pp. 71-93), suggest that parents make a child pay for duties he fails to perform. If a child fails to make his bed, put away school books, or take out the garbage, he is required to pay the family member who does it for him. The fee is small and is considered a payment for a service, not a punishment for a crime. With young children it turns out to be fun, and it helps parents avoid constantly nagging about these matters. Most important, the child learns a moral lesson. If the family decides that beds are to be made and the house is to be kept relatively neat, then a child who doesn't cooperate is failing the other family members as well as being disobedient. When children have to pay for their neglect of duties, they will soon make the connection between their actions and the cost to others. Inconsiderate and immoral persons often fail to care about the damage they do. I have heard more than one alcoholic say in defense, "I only hurt myself by my drinking." Yet, in their paths are emotionally disturbed children, depressed spouses, saddened parents, and frustrated employers. Family training needs to break down such defenses and encourage children to face the cost of sin.

Though we must be careful not to turn it into nagging, rebuke is also a useful corrective device. There are two different Hebrew words for this concept. One of them refers to checking the action of a person by a strong admonition and is translated "rebuke." "You must not drive the car without insurance." This is considered better than hidden love in Proverbs 27:5. Another word refers more to judging an act someone has done as wrong. It is translated "discipline" in 3:12 and "correction" in 6:23.

These verses do not give a parent a license to explode—to blurt out criticism or anger. Rebuke and reproof are for the benefit of the rebuked. We should avoid impulsively saying something just because we feel it—going from the lung to the tongue. When a wise father notes that his daughter's bedroom looks like it has been ransacked by a burglar, he will use his mind before his tongue. He will think about how to point out his daughter's mess without making a mess with his daughter. Rebuke, like a hypodermic needle, is sometimes necessary, but it still hurts. We should try to make it as painless as possible. Otherwise the youth puts up defenses to deal with the anger in the parent, instead of dealing with the problem being discussed. Rebukes should also be balanced with scores of compliments and encouragements. Too much criticism makes a child feel unloved. One researcher says that teenagers will feel a parent always criticizes them even when less than half the parent's comments are negative. It may take hundreds of "I love yous" to offset a few rebukes.

Discipline's Positive Side
Discipline itself is not always negative. Rewards can be given for good behavior just as painful discipline is given for bad.

God chastens His children by both pain and blessing. He taught Israel to trust Him by creating famine. But He also trained them by giving them food in the desert. "He humbled you, causing you to hunger and then feeding you with manna . . . to teach you that man does not live on bread alone but on every word that comes from the mouth of the Lord" (Deut. 8:3). The Hebrew word translated "teach" means to discipline.

Positive discipline may be more effective than negative. Rewards are powerful shapers of behavior. They don't always come in the form of candy and cookies. Activities make good incentives. Promising a boy he can play baseball after studying his math usually gets results. Grandmas discovered this long before the scientists wrote about it.

Praise can be a suitable reward if handled correctly. It should not boost the children's pride as much as their sense of usefulness. Better to say, "People enjoyed hearing you play the piano so well at the recital," than "You were the best pianist there." The goal is not to blow up children's egos by comparing them favorably with others. Besides making them feel good about their contributions to others, praise should build confidence. We should use praise to get children to do what best suits them. We should avoid saying, "We think you played perfectly in tonight's game," or, "You make me so proud," in order to push our wishes on the child. We should be careful not to use praise to enforce unrealistic standards. Saying a piano piece was played perfectly may make a child feel devastated over the little mistakes he knows he made. It may make him feel his parents will settle for nothing less than perfection. It's also unrealistic to say things like, "You're such a good girl for helping that man." Giving a little aid to someone doesn't make a person good. We should focus on the effort and the effect of what the child has done. Call these "confidence-building statements" rather than praise: "It was evident to all that you practiced a lot for the recital"; "You're really making progress"; "I know that man had an easier day because you helped him"; "Your doing the dishes made it possible for me to get more rest—thanks."

Saying, "What you did pleased me" can have some bad effects. It is proper to say that right actions please God. But God is different from parents in this regard. God's being pleased makes a behavior right. But a parent's being pleased doesn't necessarily. In fact, even with reference to God, we should stress that God is pleased because the conduct was right. Children must know that morality is not merely a matter of following the whims of their parents or even the arbitrary rule of God. An act is right because it leads to fulfillment, satisfaction, and benefit for all.

There is a specific strategy for using rewards to change a child's behavior that is especially effective. Called behavior modification, the tactic is consistent with Proverbs' teaching that good results follow good behavior. There are several steps in this process. First, identify the behavior to be changed. Here, you'll have to be specific. Resist the temptation to generalize about misbehavior. If the child jumps on the couch, we are tempted to say that he's unmanageable, instead of merely that he jumps on the couch. Behavior is best changed in bits and pieces. It's much more difficult to deal with an unmanageable child than with one who jumps on the couch. Work on stopping the furniture stomping first, then tackle other wrongdoing.

Second, identify what you want the child to do. Often, we see what we *don't* want him to do rather than what we *do* want him to do. We have to think in terms of starting something rather than stopping something. To use our example, our task is not to get the child to stop jumping on the couch, but to get him to stay on the floor. It amounts to the same thing, but the new perspective leads to a new approach.

Third, start ignoring the undesirable conduct. This is tough for those of us who feel compelled to come down with both feet on all wrongs. After a seminar on this procedure one mother said, "I find it hard to praise a child for small decreases in behavior you think should never occur at all, partly because it sounds so silly. But I'm learning to say, 'Gee, Dan, I don't think you've bitten Michael in two whole days—that's great,' and 'Look at that: you asked for an apple and you ate almost half of it all up!' " (Catherine Caldwell Brown, "It Changed My Life," *Psychology Today,* Nov. 1976, p. 48) I am not suggesting you always do this. Reproof is also effective. But at times it may be better to take attention off the wrong and place it on the right. To biblically justify this, notice how often the Proverbs stresses right behavior and the blessing, life, health, and prosperity it brings. Our stress should be on life, not death, on right, not wrong.

Fourth, instead of always catching the child being bad, start "catching" him being good. Then, give a reward. After observing your child staying off the couch for a while, offer something to make him or her feel good. A word of recognition may do: "I noticed you sat on the couch as you were supposed to and kept your feet on the floor; that is going to keep our furniture in nice shape." An activity makes a good reinforcer: "Because you came to supper on time all week you can choose your favorite game for us to play tonight." At times, a material reward might be in order, especially if offered properly. "I am so glad for your progress that I made a special batch of cookies for us." Like the old song says, "Accentuate the positive; eliminate the negative."

To make discipline effective, a parent will have to add one more strategic feature, which is found in the most famous proverb about child rearing. We'll need a whole chapter to deal with it—next.

Chapter
TWELVE

GO WITH THE GROW

Train a child according to his way
PROVERBS 22:6

"My father was a strict disciplinarian: how I appreciate him," said a friend. "My father was a strict disciplinarian: how I hate him," said another friend. Why does discipline make one child love and another hate? It all depends on how it is done.

To the Bitter End
Proverbs cautions against love without discipline. "He who spares the rod hates his son, but he who loves him is careful to discipline him" (13:24). Other biblical passages warn against discipline without love. The Apostle Paul warns fathers against harsh discipline that hurts more than it helps. "Do not exasperate your children," he writes in Ephesians 6:4. "Do not embitter your children, or they will become discouraged," he cautions in another Scripture (Col. 3:21). A parent can drive a child to rebellion or beat him down to despair. Research shows the wisdom of Paul's advice. The more severe the punishment, the more likely it is that the child will end up socially delinquent or emotionally damaged (Marvin J. Fine and Peni Holt, "Corporal Punishment in the Family: A Systems Perspective," *Psychology in the Schools,* vol. 20, Jan. 1983, p. 85).

Being authoritative instead of authoritarian is one way to avoid harming a child. The *authoritative* style of discipline has the two essentials of good discipline: control and support. On the other hand, the *authoritarian* parent neglects support, which can wreak havoc on a child's self-esteem. This kind of parent says things like, "Late for dinner—you know the rules! Get to your room without supper," or "I don't have to explain why; just do what I say." On the other hand, the authoritative parent offers some support to the growing child, "You're late for dinner; after supper you explain why and we'll decide what has to be done." Or, "I know you would like to stay up and watch that program, but I can't let you because you'd be too tired for school tomorrow." The authoritative parent, combining love and discipline, is both firm and understanding.

In child rearing, we must deal with the whole child, not merely with his conduct. Being a parent is not like being a machine that dispenses justice: when the child pushes misbehavior lever B, he automatically gets punishment X. Parents should be sensitive to the attitudes and emotions of the child, being aware of his mind and heart. No computer can tell parents exactly when they should come down hard or ease up.

One night at midnight Ginger and I were anxious and perplexed because it was an hour past the deadline for our fourteen-year-old son to be home, and he had not yet arrived. This was his first offense of this kind. Believe me, we were ready for him; after raising three other teens, we had a complete repertoire of penalties. While the clock was striking twelve, we were deciding to hear him out first and postpone the sentencing till morning. Soon after, he arrived, confessed his failure to obey, explained, but offered no excuses. Ginger and I went into conference the next morning. Should he be punished? How? Decisions like that are the toughest we have ever had to make. Considering his outstanding past record and his genuine sorrow for his lateness, we decided there would be no punishment. We settled the matter with an explanation of our decision, a warning, and an expression of our confidence in him. In this case, it turned out to be the right move, for we rarely had trouble with him.

Tailor-made Approach

Disciplining is like tailoring a suit or a dress. No pattern fits all persons. Giving each child individual attention may be what Proverbs 22:6 is telling us to do. It is possible to translate this verse, "Train a child according to his way, and when he is old he will not turn from it." The unusual Hebrew wording favors this translation, though we should not be dogmatic about such a difficult verse. If so, however, it is saying that personalized training is permanent training.

In the context of Proverbs, this makes sense. The parent should consider the type of child: naive, foolish, or wicked. If he is merely naive, he may only need a word of rebuke or instruction. If, on the other hand, he or she is one of the wicked fools described in Proverbs, the child may need spanking or other kind of punishment. Before they act, parents need to ask themselves, "Just how foolish or disobedient is my child being?"

To train "according to his way," may mean being sensitive to the developmental stages of childhood. The influential German Old Testament scholar Franz Delitzsch held this view. In 1973 he wrote, "The instruction of youth, the education of youth, ought to be conformed to the nature of youth (*Biblical Commentary on The Book of Proverbs*, vol. II, Wm. B. Eerdmans Publishing Co., p. 86). Methods of teaching and discipline should be related to the child's level of mental and physical development, he maintained. A teenager should not be treated like a toddler nor a school-age child like an adolescent. We need to gear teaching and discipline to the ability of the child to receive it.

One expert says that children are like aliens in an adult world. They hear phrases and ideas that they don't understand, so they make sense out of them the best they can. It can be very funny to find out what they made of what we said. When asked to explain his drawing of a manger scene, particularly the very heavy man beside Mary and Joseph, one little boy said, "That's round John Virgin." After drawing a plane full of passengers, another child said it was the flight to Egypt. And of course, when asked, she explained that the man in front was Pontius, the pilot.

Some misunderstandings are more serious. A student of mine asked dozens of children to draw pictures explaining what it meant to "be saved." Many of the children from evangelical homes had little idea of the biblical meaning. One little girl was typical of others. She drew a picture of a small girl and what appeared to be a goat in a pasture. **Dots** that covered the sky were rain, she told us. God saved the little girl just when the goat was about to buck her by causing rain that made the goat leave.

Though we can't prevent children from hearing things they will misconstrue, we can aim our teaching to their levels of understanding and use curriculum that does that. Parents can help by asking their children lots of questions. "What is salvation? forgiveness? love?" Or ask them to put their ideas into drawings, such as a picture of God, or their ideas of death. We might spare them some hard times by discovering and correcting their wrong ideas. A little child might go through months of fear because of a misunderstanding about God's wrath or feel funny about being naked because God and the angels are watching.

Talking and praying with children is crucial to understanding them. Imagine my surprise when one of my children prayed that his grandmother would soon make it out of purgatory. "My club leader taught us about that place," he said later. A few weeks before, purgatory had been mentioned in a talk, I discovered--to criticize, not condone it. My boy had misunderstood. Regular conversation may be the most effective means of teaching a child "according to his way."

Besides our instruction, discipline should be geared to the

child's level of development. The amount of direct control should change, permitting the child to make more of his decisions as he grows older. The teen needs some freedom to decide and fail, to learn from his own mistakes. A child needs to learn to be independent because he is given more autonomy as he grows up. As children do more and more outside the home, it becomes virtually impossible for parents to have direct control over them. The father of one fourteen-year-old said of his daughter, "I feel like the circle of her life is widening away from us." If parents are too strict, children may run away or rebel in destructive ways. To prepare them for responsible independence, parents must give up control slowly and systematically as children are able to handle it.

Parents will have countless dilemmas over exactly how much freedom should be given and when. "My thirteen-year-old daughter wants to sleep overnight at a friend's house—should I permit it?" is a situation submitted to me in one of my seminars. A number of things should be considered in situations like this. First, the parent must decide when the child needs protection from predicaments he or she isn't yet equipped to handle. Spending the night in someone else's home can pose a lot of threats to the child's welfare. Parents of a thirteen-year-old should insist they first know the friend's family before granting permission. This may be difficult in neighborhoods where parents are not easily informed about the child's schoolmates' homes. This is typically difficult for families that are new in the area. Parents should not be embarrassed about visiting the friend's home and learning all they can before permitting their son or daughter to spend time there. Families would do well to create networks of families who know each other well enough to entrust their children to one another for these excursions away from home. Secondly, the parent must think about how the child feels. We know that kids in their early teens want their parents' control even though they may seem to resent it. They are often afraid of situations but are too threatened by their peers to say no. They feel relieved when the parent says no for them. Experts say that teens are more secure when the parents create clearly understood boundaries that keep them from harm but permit enough freedom for them to grow.

Parents should dose out responsibility as the child shows himself responsible. Disciplining teens is not a matter of simply laying down the law. David Elkind, one of the major authorities in the field of child development, suggests we view parent-teen relationships as a series of contracts. The first type of contract focuses on freedom and responsibility. Parents give more liberty to the more trustworthy. Use of the family car can be connected to effort at doing schoolwork, for example: Elkind believes parents today too freely bestow freedom on irresponsible kids.

The second type of contract deals with loyalty and commitment. Parents expect their children to remain loyal to values and beliefs they hold, while in turn, teens can count on parents to live out those values as much as possible. What's good for the little goose is good for the big gander. When parents try to force standards they don't hold on the child, they undermine their moral training efforts. It is a good rule for parents not to impose more discipline than what they themselves live out. Studies of families confirm that when parents hold their children to values they themselves don't live by, the children will usually fall far short of their parents' expectations. Parents are most effective communicators of values when the standards they teach are the ones they practice (Bruno Bettelheim, "Punishment vs. Discipline," *The Atlantic*, Nov. 1985, pp. 54, 56). Achievement and support make up the third type of contract. When a parent expects success at school or loyal effort in practicing a sport or musical instrument, the parent pledges to provide what is necessary: money, transportation, and emotional support.

One of the reasons children need higher degrees of freedom as they grow is that they need to eventually separate from their parents. This distancing of teens from their parents, called differentiation, doesn't necessarily mean they will depart from all their parents' values, beliefs, and ways. Rather it involves their becoming separate and distinct enough to establish their own identities. If parents push too hard to recreate themselves in their children, the children either rebel or give in. When they surrender to their parents' wishes, they fail to establish their own personal senses of self. This could cause problems later, in the early thirties or in mid-life, when they feel cheated that they have not become what they really wanted or were meant to be. One of the young women in our church shocked us by becoming unfaithful to her husband. Raised in a Christian home, an exemplary believer, she seemed an unlikely candidate to be an adulteress. In the process of trying to restore her to fellowship, the pastor and deacons found her in a state of rebellion, saying she had always conformed to her parents' wishes. Now she wanted to be herself.

Thankfully, through the love and support of her husband and others she returned to her husband and her faith. It's possible her actions were based on what the professionals call "identity foreclosure." During her adolescence, she failed to find herself.

When parents demand too much conformity, a child may not give in, but rebel. This can be unfortunate because the child does not really find his own identity, but establishes a false one, a "reaction identity." The adolescent angrily becomes what his parents are not. Suppose a parent allows a teen few choices. It's as if they are saying, "We are blue and you must be blue, just like us." Suppose, however, it's within God's will that the child be purple, like his parents in most ways, but distinct, "according to his way." Parents must give enough freedom for the child to make this "differentiation." Bound too tightly, the child revolts. Instead of purple, he chooses to be yellow. This is a problem, not merely because the teen is different from the parent, but because he is different because of the parent. God didn't make him to be yellow; it's an identity born of a resentful backlash. Some kids do drugs, change religions, become delinquent, and go to different extremes to differentiate themselves from their parents.

To prevent rebellion or identity foreclosure, parents need to decide where to give their child room to grow, such as in areas that don't involve morality. It's not always easy to draw a moral line, though. Take contemporary music as an example. Some Christians tell parents to forbid their teen's listening to rock music because the rhythm is sinful. Yet it may be far better for parents to teach children to discern between the good and the bad lyrics instead of taking an all-or-nothing approach to the music that is so much a part of the teen world. On his radio program James Dobson answered a caller who wanted to know if it was proper to make all TV programs off limits to her children, as her pastor wanted her to do. "Do you mean all TV—including Sesame Street and other educational programs?" he asked. "Yes," she replied. "Lady, I wouldn't do that. If you deprive your children of their cultural heritage, someday they are going to grow up and throw those rules back in your face." Dobson is right; we must be sure that in our efforts to protect the children we don't deprive them, making them turn against us later.

If they do rebel, we should not deny them our love. Children will most closely follow parents who display a combination of teaching, example, and love. In our efforts of discipline, we should not withdraw our love or threaten to do so. Unconditional love becomes an issue particularly in the case of a rebellious teenager. Parents are caught between defending their own morals and expressing their natural affection. In this battle, some parents believe they must give in to values and reject the child who has left the Christian faith, become a homosexual, or turned into a delinquent. But even in these cases it seems best not to betray the natural love tie. If, after a teen builds a wall between himself and his parents, the parents also build a wall, then two walls must be broken down if that son or daughter is to be reconciled. When parents keep the door of their love open, they are maintaining the greatest avenue of influence they have on the child. Not that love includes giving in to the teen, providing money or other support for his or her damaging activities. Sometimes love must be tough, withholding and denying supports. Parents can refuse without rejecting. Like the father of the prodigal son, they can pour out their affection no matter what far country the child might wander to.

What's Not So Apparent About a Parent

To train a child "according to his way," most of us parents need to learn more about why we parent as we do. Knowing what to do is less our problem than doing it. Give a blank sheet to most parents, ask them to write six guidelines for child rearing, and most would quickly write ten--good ones. Most would also confess they don't do them very well. Our problem is that we know more about what makes our children tick than we do what makes us tock. We know, for example, that when a teen comes home after the local curfew that we should meet him at the door and carefully hear all explanations, calmly discuss it, and decide what action to take. Why is it then that halfway into the explanations, we blow our stacks, and scatter sarcastic words and immature accusations all over the place. I know a man who has been yelling at his kids for over fifteen years. He confesses that his short temper has not only alienated some of his children, but taught them to yell right back. In his case, he didn't need another book about kids, he needed a book about parents. The same may be true of parents who are too strict or unloving. If those parents can find out *why*, they may be in a better position to do something about it.

There are a number of places to search for an answer to irrational parenting. Sometimes our parenting is most shaped by the past, particularly our childhood home life. A parent, for example, who is most likely to overreact to his adolescent's misbehavior is one who rebelled as a teenager. Remembering the confusion, the unhappiness, the hurt, he or she is desperate to keep his child from walking the same path. Any little move toward independence taken by the teenager looks like an act of rebellion and the parent comes down heavy-handedly (Strommen and Strommen, *Five Cries*, p. 16). Such parents can make the connection between their own past and their tactics with their children, learning to ease off and to be more moderate and sensible.

Parents who were abused when they were children will have particular struggles with parenting. One mother told of her fear that she would treat her boy as her father treated her. She explained a complex chain of influence. Dad was never close to her or warm. Criticism was his game. He seemed indifferent and angry all of the time. Even when she visits home as a grown daughter, he takes no time to stop and talk; her visits usually end up in arguments. Her efforts at emotional bridge building have failed, leaving an empty place in her heart. But during all these years, she had not taken his abuse sitting down. Some children withdraw into themselves, accepting the criticism and wallowing in self-pity or painful self-hate, but she defended herself by lashing back. Standing up to him had turned her into a domineering, critical person herself. She couldn't accept rebukes gracefully. Any time she was under a boss who acted like her father, she fought back. What worried her when she talked with me was this: how would she react when her son reached the age of two and began to defy her? Could she keep an even temper? Would she lash out at him as she had done to her father? There's hope for this woman because she is aware of influences she can deal with. Many parents don't grapple with these influences because they don't know about them.

Parents who are especially vulnerable to dominating their kids are those who have been deeply hurt by unfulfilled dreams. Often they want to live out those dreams through their children. A father whose injury kept him from playing college football may unmercifully press his son to excel in sports. A blue-collar worker who flunked out of college may say to his son, "I goofed off in school, and I worked in a factory all my life; I'm not going to let that happen to you."

If Proverbs 22:6 does mean we should train a child "according to his way," we should be certain not to confuse that with shaping them in *our* way.

It may not be the past as much as present circumstances that are affecting how you handle your kids. We know, for example, that child abuse statistics rise with the unemployment figures. Parents without jobs often turn into parents without normal self-restraint, taking out their frustration and anger on their children. Other stressful circumstances, like the death of a family member, divorce and separation, financial burden, and a heavy schedule can drastically affect the way persons handle parenting if they aren't careful.

Our emotional state can play a major part. Many parents discipline out of sheer fear. Once when we were in the Philippines as missionaries, my wife, Ginger, and I were hit by a severe case of parental anxiety. In the Christian school attended by our children bad news broke out: a number of teens were caught doing drugs. Emotional tremors spread through parents all over our city. Questions were asked; trust between parents and children was tested. What shook us was the fact that one of the boys in trouble was our son's best friend. Though teachers assured us that our son was not among the guilty, we were still among the frightened. One late afternoon, our fears were confirmed. Our son did not arrive home on the school bus. Our daughter Becky told us he had gotten out midway during the hour-long drive home. What would make him disobediently get off the bus in the middle of metropolitan Manila? Our dread mixed with doubt and anger, which made us think the worst.

For fifteen years I've felt badly about how I overreacted when he got home. I turned his domestic felony into a capital crime. My intense questioning filled the air with mistrust. For weeks afterward we watched him like private detectives. Fear had turned parents into prosecutors. We were afraid for him, that he was in big trouble, and fearful for ourselves, that we were failures. His only explanation was that he felt like getting off the bus and going to the shopping center. We only learned what he was up to a few years ago. I asked my now grown, married son, to solve the mystery for us. Remember when you left the bus? Why did you do it? Was it drugs? A girl, maybe. "No, Dad, I just felt like it. Perhaps I was trying to be a little independent." I laughed when he told me, wishing I had had more sense of humor then.

Fear can force parents to imagine wild fantasies of what their kids are up to, pushing them to be ultrasuspicious, overstrict, and overprotective at the least sign of strangeness. The problem is that when children become teens, they do strange things without being in deep trouble. A thirteen-year-old boy wants a transistor radio like everyone else. His parents refuse on financial grounds. Two days later he comes home with one; when asked where he got it, he says he traded something for it with one of the kids at school. He refuses to say more. Or a fourteen-year-old girl comes to her mother sobbing, saying that she has just ripped a button off the blouse she was going to wear. Her mother says, "Oh, I'm sorry. I'll sew it for you." The daughter turns away, slamming the door, saying, "You don't really care" (Ellen Galinsky, *Between Generations*, Time Books, 1981, p. 229). Any little deviation will send some parents into panicsville. Much of this panic is due to the parents' deep dread of failure. Of fourteen worries listed in one survey, none drew as high a rating as the worry over "the job I am doing in raising this child" (Strommen and Strommen, *Five Cries*, p. 16). Because so much of our self-esteem is bound up in our children, we tend to interpret their failures as our failures. A little trouble and we moan, "We shouldn't have been so strict, or maybe we were too lenient." "Why did we let him buy that first rock record?" "Why didn't we spend more time with her?" Our fear mixes with guilt to fuse into a horrible basis for disciplining. Granted, parents should be alert for alarms that signal serious trouble. But we cannot justify doing anything out of anxiety, even when it concerns our children. "Do not be anxious about anything," said Paul (Phil. 4:6). Faith, not fear, must direct parents. Above all we must trust God for our children; and we must put confidence in the past training we have given them, despite the mistakes made, not permitting irrational fear to turn us into suspicious inquisitors instead of loving parents. We must move ahead in hope, not be bogged down in the past and in guilt.

When Wisdom Is in Your Future
Possibly the most prominent unseen enemy stalking our modern homes is fear. We may not talk about it much, but we are afraid. Parents fear their children will go astray; husbands and wives fear their marriages will go wrong. Young children lie awake in the darkness, overhearing the angry voices of their quarreling parents, wondering if they will still be a family tomorrow.

Fear is like a sour odor that lingers in our hearts and homes, but there is something that will drive it away: hope. Fear sees the future as a dark, dismal tunnel littered with unsolvable problems and unhappiness. Hope views the future as a lighted corridor, strewn with trouble perhaps, but brightened by the prospect that God will triumph. The Book of Proverbs is filled with a hope bred by faith. "Have no fear of sudden disaster... for the Lord will be your confidence" (3:25-26).

Many years ago a friend who is a professional counselor said this: "Whenever anyone comes to you for counseling, the first thing you should attempt to do is to offer them hope." Throughout this book, I've tried to do that, because I know what it is to wrestle with hopelessness and fear. If I have explained the proverbs accurately and you have studied them carefully, we should both have greater optimism. This hope is one of the promised rewards of true wisdom: "If you find it [wisdom], there is a future hope for you, and your hope will not be cut off" (24:14).